Biological Weapons: Weapons of the Future?

SIGNIFICANT ISSUES SERIES papers are written for and published by the Center for Strategic and International Studies.
Series Editors: David M. Abshire
                  Douglas M. Johnston, Jr.
Director of Studies: Erik R. Peterson
Director of Publications: Nancy B. Eddy
Managing Editor: Roberta L. Howard
Associate Editor: Yoma Ullman

The Center for Strategic and International Studies
1800 K Street, N.W., Suite 400
Washington, D.C. 20006
Telephone: (202) 887-0200
Telex: 7108229583
Fax: (202) 775-3199
Cable Address: CENSTRAT

Volume XV, Number 1

Significant Issues Series

Biological Weapons
Weapons of the Future?

edited by Brad Roberts

foreword by Glen Browder

The Center for Strategic
and International Studies
Washington, D.C.

Library of Congress Cataloging-in-Publication Data

Biological weapons : weapons of the future? / edited by Brad Roberts ;
   foreword by Glen Browder.
       p.   cm. — (Significant issues series, ISSN 0736-7136 ; v. 15, no. 1)
   ISBN 0-89206-210-X
   1. Biological weapons. I. Roberts, Brad. II. Series.
   UG447.8.B57 1993
   358'.3882—dc20   92-47356
                                                                                CIP

Contents

About the Contributors

Glen Browder is a member of Congress (D-Ala.). As a member of the House Armed Services Committee, he chaired an inquiry into the chemical and biological weapons problem that in January 1993 made a comprehensive set of policy recommendations.

W. Seth Carus is director for defense strategy on the Policy Planning Staff in the Office of the Secretary of Defense.

Thomas Dashiell is a consultant to the U.S. Arms Control and Disarmament Agency (ACDA).

David L. Huxsoll served previously as commander of the U.S. Army's Medical Research Institute of Infectious Diseases (USAMRID) at Fort Detrick and is now associate dean of the School of Veterinary Sciences at Louisiana State University.

Robert H. Kupperman is a senior adviser to CSIS. A former chief scientist at ACDA, he has also served in the Office of Emergency Preparedness in the Executive Office of the President.

Michael Moodie was assistant director for multilateral affairs of ACDA at the time this chapter was written.

Graham S. Pearson is director general of the British Chemical and Biological Defence Establishment, Porton Down.

Brad Roberts is a research fellow at CSIS where he also serves as editor of *The Washington Quarterly*.

David M. Smith is a scientist at the Los Alamos National Laboratory.

Victor A. Utgoff is deputy director of the Strategy, Forces, and Resources Division of the Institute for Defense Analyses.

Foreword

As the House Armed Services Committee reviewed the results of the Persian Gulf War and began to assess the requirements for the U.S. military in the post–cold war world, some of us quickly grew very concerned about the potential threat posed by the proliferation of chemical and biological weapons (cbw). As Director of Central Intelligence Robert Gates noted in testimony to the committee's Defense Policy Panel in December 1991,

> the accelerating proliferation of nuclear, biological, and chemical weapons in other countries around the world is probably of gravest concern. The more countries that possess such weapons—even if acquired for deterrent purposes—the greater the likelihood that such weapons will be used.

The almost heroic effort of U.S. forces to ensure that they were prepared to survive and sustain operations in the Gulf under the threat of Iraqi chemical and biological attack was a tribute to the team assembled there. But it was also an indictment of the generally low readiness of U.S. forces to cope with battle in a contaminated environment, despite the increasing salience of the cbw threat and the steady flow of funds for this purpose in recent years.

These concerns about chemical and biological warfare vulnerabilities and about the general place of the cbw problem in the larger set of U.S. defense and security priorities in the 1990s were shared by committee chairman Les Aspin (D-Wis.). Believing that the committee needed to take decisive action in the cbw area, he directed that I chair an inquiry into the nature of the chemical and biological weapons threat and the ways that we as a nation might counter it, with Martin Lancaster (D-N.C.) and Larry Hopkins (R-Ky.) as the other members of the inquiry.

Working through the issues related to chemical weapons (cw) proved relatively straightforward for the inquiry because we were able quickly to uncover a wealth of information, expertise, and opinion with which to conduct our inquiry. But such assets proved more elusive in the biological area. There is generally less information available about biological than chemical weapons, and much of the relevant information is classified (hence our reliance on it would limit our ability to debate our recommendations publicly). Expertise on issues of biological warfare defense and the associated policy questions is narrowly focused, and we found no track record of extensive public analysis and debate. Opinions proved strong, which was not surprising given the moral abhorrence we all share toward biological weapons.

To help us focus the inquiry's efforts on biological weapons (bw) and to draw out the best available expertise, we turned to the Center for Strategic and International Studies and research fellow Brad Roberts, whose track record of providing analysis and support to interested members of Congress on the chemical arms control issue was well known to many of us. The result was a one-day symposium at CSIS on November 4, 1992, designed to bring together around one table a selection of people with different areas of expertise for an exchange of views on new challenges to U.S. bw defense policy.

This volume includes papers prepared for that symposium, subsequently revised to take account of the discussion. They are being published as part of our general commitment to help raise the level of debate about U.S. biological warfare defense policy choices. The views included here are necessarily those of the authors presenting them.

An overview of the biological warfare issue and a historical perspective on policy is provided in the first two chapters. The opening essay describes the genesis of U.S. thinking about the bw problem. The second chapter offers a British perspective, highlighting areas of convergence and divergence in the views of our two countries.

The following three essays describe and evaluate new challenges to bw defense policies, including proliferation, technological change, and bioterrorism. Our discussions benefited also from a presentation by Matthew Meselson about his recent trip to Sverdlovsk (now Ekaterinburg) to investigate the 1979 anthrax outbreak there; because of a prior commitment to publish his findings elsewhere, this volume does not include his presentation.

A discussion of future policy priorities is provided in the last three chapters. One emphasizes military policy choices. The second focuses on the arms control agenda and the difficult issues associated with strengthening the Biological and Toxin Weapons Convention. The final chapter, by volume editor Brad Roberts, is a comprehensive review of the subject, tying together the various historical and policy discussions into a broad review of current policy choices.

On behalf of my colleagues in the inquiry and the House Armed Services Committee, I would like to thank CSIS and Brad Roberts for their efforts in support of our inquiry. Financial support for their work was made possible through a grant from the William and Flora Hewlett Foundation, and I would like to express the gratitude of everyone involved in this project for the Foundation's generous assistance.

The inquiry is reporting its findings and recommendations to the Defense Policy Panel and the full committee and looks forward to sharing and debating them with the defense policy community when the new administration and Congress begin their urgent work in 1993.

The title of this volume poses the essential question: Are biological weapons the weapons of the future? They probably are not. The proliferation of such weapons and the continued threat of terrorist use should alert us to the risks in this area and to the changing international political context of policy. But they should not induce hysteria. Nor should the increasingly evident shortcomings of the arms control regime. The bw problem is growing more challenging in many ways, but there is little evidence that it has somehow slipped out of control or that the basic focus of policy should be drastically changed.

We hope that this small volume will contribute to the achievement of more effective policy in this area. The scourge of biological warfare will not quickly be eliminated from relations among nations. But with a clearer focus on policy priorities and concerted leadership by the United States, there is a real possibility that the 1990s will be a decade in which fears of this problem will ease rather than grow worse.

Glen Browder
U.S. House of Representatives
December 15, 1992

1
A Review of U.S. Biological Warfare Policies
Thomas Dashiell

In preparing a comprehensive overview of the biological warfare and defense programs and policies of the United States it is crucial that the activities and related policies be portrayed in the context of the times and circumstances in which they occurred. The policy of the United States regarding biological warfare has been remarkably consistent since its initial development. Between 1941 and 1969 the policy was first to deter the use of biological weapons (bw) against the United States and its forces, and, second, to retaliate if deterrence failed. As a result of President Richard Nixon's ban on all biological and toxin weapons, their destruction, and the subsequent development of the Biological and Toxin Weapons Convention (BWC) in 1972 and its adoption by the United States, the nation has since 1969 maintained only a defensive program as a deterrent.

Fundamental to the development of a deterrent strategy has been thorough study and analysis of U.S. vulnerability to both overt and covert bw attacks and continual examination of a full range of retaliatory options. Recognition by U.S. scientists of the potential of biological weapons prompted the start of the program in World War II. Before the war, only the Geneva Protocol of 1925 (for the Prohibition of the Use in War of Asphyxiating, Poisonous or Other Gases, and of Bacteriological Methods of Warfare) served as a control on bacteriological methods of warfare. The United States signed the Protocol in 1925, but it was not ratified until 1975.

Because a potential bw threat still exists and the convention is not effectively verifiable—nor do we know any way to make it so—the United States continues to maintain a defensive program as a deterrent. This program has as its primary objective the development and fielding of an adequate level of protection for U.S. forces against the use of biological and toxin weapons. Its second objective is to provide a highly visible deterrent to any potential use through this defensive

1

posture. Such a highly visible deterrent is one key purpose of the present Biological Defense Research Program; since its inception the openness and transparency of the program has been paramount. Annual unclassified reports have been provided to the Congress and the public that detail the activities and costs of the program. Cooperative long-term research efforts with other countries and the civil public health programs of the United States and other countries give the effort further transparency. Indeed, the confidence-building measures (CBMs) agreed at the Second Review Conference of the BWC in September 1986 were an effort to bring all parties to the convention up to the same level of openness that the U.S. program has displayed. At the Third Review Conference the CBMs were expanded and enhanced by the addition of four new measures designed to increase the openness and transparency of the programs of all parties.

Historical Overview

A brief history of the U.S. program may be useful in understanding current policy issues. In 1941, Henry Stimson, at that time secretary of war, requested the National Academy of Sciences to evaluate the bw situation. The Academy concluded that biological weapons were feasible and recommended that steps be taken to reduce the vulnerability of the United States to attacks using them. In 1942, the first research and development program was initiated to prepare defensive measures. In 1943, Camp Detrick was established, its construction was begun, and the program was broadened to include bw agents and a field trial program. During World War II, the policy on biological weapons implicitly paralleled that on chemical weapons (cw), that is, retaliation against use by others. At the end of the war in 1945, all work was phased down to research only. From 1946 to 1950, planning was conducted under the authority of the Research and Development Board of the Office of the Secretary of Defense. It was again found that the United States was very susceptible to bw attack, and goals, objectives, and an organization were developed for a program to remedy this. During this period, small-scale outdoor testing with simulants was initiated but there was no human volunteer testing. From the end of World War II until 1950, no production was carried out for the purpose of operational readiness and no facilities were available for such work.

During the Korean War years (1950–1953), a production facility was constructed at Pine Bluff Arsenal, large area vulnerability testing was begun (for example, San Francisco), and anticrop systems were developed and produced. In 1950, the president continued the policy of retaliation only. In 1951, the secretary of defense reviewed the program and increased work in all areas; the defensive program was almost doubled in the next year.

From 1954 to 1959, the cold war years, production of bw agents was conducted at Pine Bluff and the vaccine research program was expanded to include the use of human volunteers. The policy was revised to include preparation for the use of chemical or biological weapons to enhance military effectiveness. The Defense Science Board reviewed the program and recommended increased research and the development of a use doctrine. During the limited war years, 1959 to 1962, the Pentagon's director of Defense Research and Engineering (DDR&E) recommended a five-year expansion of the program. An incapacitating agent program was initiated and a comprehensive program plan developed. The anticrop program was restarted, the production plant expanded, and the development of effective vaccines for Q fever and tularemia allowed their standardization as agents. Deseret Test Center was established to conduct joint tests. During the Vietnam War years (1963–1968), production and filling of various agents into munitions continued at Pine Bluff, production of anticrop agent continued, production and use of chemical herbicides was begun, as was production of enterotoxin. Defensive programs emphasized detection systems, vaccine programs, and improved prophylaxis and therapy.

The U.S. BW Program and the BWC

The disarmament and phase-down portion of the program began in November 1969, when President Nixon unilaterally renounced all biological weapons and extended the ban to include toxins in February 1970. From May 1971 to March

1973, all antipersonnel stocks and their related munitions and all anticrop materials were destroyed at a total disposal cost of $14.7 million. In April 1972, the United States signed the Biological and Toxin Weapons Convention, which was approved by the U.S. Senate in December 1974 and ratified by President Gerald Ford in January 1975.

Following these actions, the program was reconstituted for biological defense only. It was largely in-house and concentrated on vaccines, prophylaxis and therapy, and detection. In 1980, the weakness of the program and the impact of the rapid growth in biotechnology with its potential for changing biological weapons was recognized in a Defense Science Board study, as was the threat of proliferation. A number of changes had occurred since the signature of the BWC including the natural occurrence of diseases such as Lassa fever, Legionnaires' disease, and hemorrhagic fevers such as ebola (all potential agents), and the use of mycotoxins in Southeast Asia. These developments resulted in the completion of new threat assessments by 1983. As a result, funding was increased, university roles expanded, and new avenues of detection and warning and a more generic medical research program approach initiated. A key feature of the program is its openness and transparency and its complete adherence to the BWC and the convention's CBMs.

The decision by the United States to maintain a defensive program while a party to the BWC has inspired much discussion. When President Nixon renounced all biological warfare, a determination had been made that U.S. intelligence was sufficient to safeguard U.S. security interests and that biological weapons had limited military utility. Signing the BWC, which required that other treaty parties relinquish their biological weapons, could only enhance U.S. security. Indeed, Dr. Fred Iklé, then director of the U.S. Arms Control and Disarmament Agency, testifying in 1974 in favor of the ratification of the BWC before the House Committee on Armed Services, said:

> It has been our decision that it was in our net interest to have this agreement [the BWC] even though, in a strict sense, it is not very fully verifiable. Why? It is not only

because biological weapons are so undesirable from a moral point of view but because it is very dubious what role they would play in a military manner and for military purposes. It does seem to be in our net interest to rather dampen the competition in biological weapons.

Herein lies the paradox of verification and the BWC. Treaty violations are extremely difficult to detect with any certainty. Note the controversy that still surrounds the accidental release of anthrax that occurred in Sverdlovsk in the former USSR in April 1979. Note also the fact that the president of the Russian Republic has now admitted that a biological warfare research program continued in his country until March 1992.

Cheating on the BWC, however, generally does not create a situation that threatens the strategic balance; the United States has a wide variety of nonbiological weapon systems with which to respond. This is not, however, necessarily the case for nonnuclear states or some developing countries, which means that proliferation is a very real problem.

New Challenges

Also of extreme importance are the many advances that have occurred in biotechnology in the years since the BWC was signed. Most practical people will agree that the ability to engineer novel agents with specific characteristics designed to overcome problems of stability, infectivity, toxicity, and production has added to the problems of detection and its role in verification. Indeed, the ability to produce large quantities of biological agents and toxin rapidly through bioengineering makes the problem of storage of agents moot but at the same time makes detection through national technical means much more difficult. This is a primary reason why effective verification is so difficult.

Today proliferation of biological and toxin weapons has increased as well as that of chemical weapons, especially in some areas of the world. Note the concerns of the Allied forces about the bw threat during the 1990–1991 war in the Persian Gulf. If a party or a nonparty to the BWC decides to cheat, it will probably easily avoid detection. The very real improvements possible through biotechnology in the military utility of biological weapons, or even any perceived improvements, increase the likelihood that a country will risk violation of the BWC. This problem is confounded by the dual-use nature of the equipment and technology used for both legitimate medical research and biological weapons.

A significant deficiency in the current U.S. bw defensive posture is the lack of definitive, rapid, accurate systems of detection that can be used in the field both for detection of illegal activities and for verification of perceived breaches of the treaty. Once it is recognized that any charges of violation must withstand legal challenges while not revealing any intelligence information, the scope of the problem can be developed. It is possible that many of the same biotechnological processes that can be used to subvert the treaty can be applied to the problems of detection and verification. Until that point is reached, improvements in the CBMs, better adherence by all parties, and improving trust in the present treaty parameters is the only practical avenue to follow. Indeed, the response to the earlier measures agreed at the Second Review Conference and those now embodied in the third has not been good (only 30 responses as of fall 1992). Understanding that these measures are not legally binding but only politically binding does not change the situation dramatically. If a country wants to make the BWC work, it will participate under any circumstances, with or without effective verification.

2
Biological Weapons: The British View

Graham S. Pearson

In the United Kingdom, attention focused on biological warfare in the early years of World War II when Axis activities in that field caused concern. After the war, biological weapons (bw) were seen as a major priority until the late 1950s, when the UK offensive biological program ceased.

The United Kingdom was a codepositary of the Biological and Toxin Weapons Convention (BWC) of 1972. Following the signing of that convention, the Microbiological Research Establishment of the Ministry of Defence was transferred, in 1979, to the Department of Health to become the Centre for Applied Microbiology and Research in the Public Health Laboratory Service. The later 1970s saw an increasing concern about biological warfare, the potential for increased producibility of agents, and the manipulation of agents arising from biotechnology.

In the mid-1980s, this increased concern resulted in the provision of additional resources for biological defense. When the Persian Gulf conflict of late 1990 and early 1991 occurred, with the threat that Iraq might use biological weapons against the coalition forces, the United Kingdom was well placed to deploy at least some expedient biological detection and medical countermeasures.

The completion of the negotiations in Geneva on the Chemical Weapons Convention (CWC) and the experiences of the United Nations (UN) Security Council Special Commission on Iraq have increased the awareness of states in respect to the hazard from biological weapons and the need to improve the BWC by considering a possible verification regime. This paper elaborates on the background to the current UK position, which seeks to make the most of the present window of opportunity to improve and strengthen the BWC.

Historical Perspective, 1940–1972

The dark years of World War II saw an increasing concern in the United Kingdom that Germany and Japan might be contemplating the use of biological warfare. Accordingly, in 1940, the Biology Department, Porton was established as a separate autonomous organization to investigate the feasibility of biological warfare and to develop a means of retaliation should biological weapons be used against British forces.

This led in 1942–1943 to trials on Gruinard Island in the Northwest of Scotland, which demonstrated that anthrax spores disseminated into the atmosphere from bombs were effective in killing sheep tethered downwind. There was very close collaboration between the United Kingdom, the United States, and Canada throughout World War II. By the end of the war, the UK retaliatory capability comprised 5 million cattle cakes impregnated with anthrax. These were to be disseminated through the flare chutes of British aircraft over Germany should biological weapons be used against the United Kingdom.

At the end of World War II, this retaliatory capability was destroyed. The importance and significance of biological warfare led to the building of the Microbiological Research Establishment on a site adjacent to the then Chemical Defence Experimental Establishment at Porton Down. It is important to remember that this large new building was built at a time of great austerity in postwar Britain and represented a considerable investment in what was then seen as a weapon of considerable significance.

The late 1950s saw the unilateral decision by the United Kingdom to abandon both chemical and biological weapons (cbw). The decision was taken in the light of the politico-economic situation of that time. East-West cold war was then of major concern and nuclear deterrence was seen as the vital element of national defense strategy. Since that date, Porton Down has been solely concerned with the provision of effective protective measures for members of the British Armed Forces. Meanwhile, across the Atlantic, arising from the collaboration in World War II, the U.S. retaliatory program continued unabated. When this program ceased in 1969, a number of agents had been type classified and a range of delivery means were in service.

The World of 1972

In 1972 there was no doubt about the utility of biological warfare, which had been proven by all means short of actual use in war. The UN secretary general had issued a report in 1969 that had shown that biological weapons had a potential strategic impact parallel to that of nuclear weapons. In addition, evidence available to the UN secretary general had shown that biological weapons were far cheaper than conventional, chemical, or nuclear weapons.

At that stage, the East-West cold war was near its peak and the West had long depended upon nuclear means to deter aggression. This, then, was the background to the signing of the BWC in 1972 with the United Kingdom, the United States, and the USSR as codepositaries. This convention for the first time banned the development and production of a whole class of weapons. The provisions for compliance and verification matched the norm of the period.

The Next Two Decades, 1972–1992

The decades from 1972 to 1992 saw the advent of biotechnology with its prospects for the enhanced producibility of biological warfare agents as well as the potential for genetic manipulation. In addition, just before the First Review Conference of the BWC in 1979, reports emerged of the incident involving anthrax spores at Sverdlovsk (Ekaterinburg). The Western view was always that this incident had resulted from an accident in a military facility, resulting in the release of anthrax spores into the atmosphere and the consequential death of several civilians through inhaling the spores. It is interesting that although the official Soviet Union explanation of the deaths was contaminated black market meat, in the last couple of years investigative reporting in the former Soviet Union and now in Russia has demonstrated that pulmonary anthrax occurred in Sverdlovsk and was associated with an

Figure 1
Threat Spectrum of Chemical and Biological Weapons

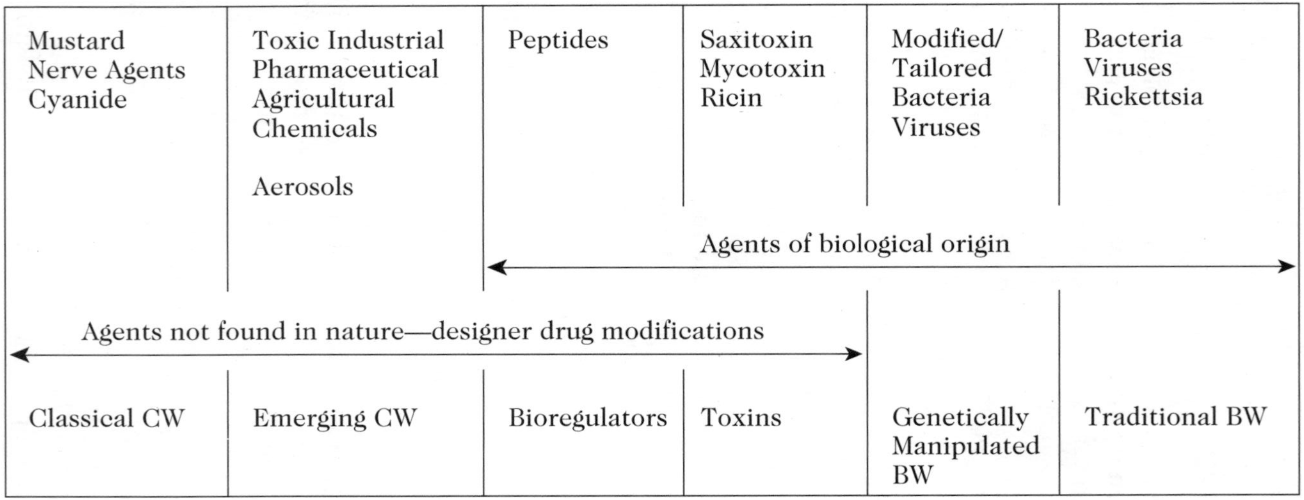

Mustard Nerve Agents Cyanide	Toxic Industrial Pharmaceutical Agricultural Chemicals Aerosols	Peptides	Saxitoxin Mycotoxin Ricin	Modified/ Tailored Bacteria Viruses	Bacteria Viruses Rickettsia
Classical CW	Emerging CW	Bioregulators	Toxins	Genetically Manipulated BW	Traditional BW

Agents of biological origin

Agents not found in nature—designer drug modifications

KEY POINTS

1. Potential CBW threat spectrum is broad and extends well beyond the agents of WW I vintage.
2. Toxicity increases from left to right.
3. The feasibility of using such weapons has increased, as has the ability to produce the agent in quantity.

accident in a military institute. The contaminated black
market meat explanation is now thoroughly discredited.

The early 1980s saw the yellow rain incident in Southeast
Asia. Although there has been much debate about yellow rain
and what was actually used, much remains unclear, which
underlines the need to take the problem of the proliferation of
chemical and biological weapons seriously. The increased
concern about both yellow rain and the Sverdlovsk anthrax
incident led to appreciation in the mid-1980s of the potential
chemical and biological warfare spectrum (figure 1). This
spectrum spreads from the classical chemical weapons (cw)
agents such as the nerve agents and mustard, through emerging chemical warfare agents, to the mid-spectrum agents
comprising bioregulators and toxins, to the biological warfare
agents and their genetically manipulated variants.

The appreciation of the potential cbw spectrum resulted in
emphasis being placed by the defense community on broad-
band protective measures effective against as much of the
spectrum as possible. In addition, increased attention was paid
to biological defense, which had largely been allowed to lapse
in the years following the signing of the BWC.

The other development of the 1980s was the increasing
proliferation of cbw possessors around the world. By the end of
the decade, some 20 nations or more were assessed to possess
or to be seeking to acquire chemical weapons, while some 10
nations were assessed to have or to be seeking to acquire
biological weapons.

The decade ended with the Persian Gulf conflict in late
1990 and early 1991 when Iraq invaded Kuwait. The coalition
forces faced a very real threat of both chemical and biological
weapons and this fact served to concentrate minds wonder-
fully. The Persian Gulf War necessitated the deployment of
expedient measures to provide a detection and medical countermeasures capability against the biological warfare agents
that Iraq was assessed to have. The end of the war and the
creation of the UN Special Commission under Security Council
Resolution 687 resulted in specialist inspections of Iraq's
assessed bw capabilities. These inspections have to date forced
Iraq to declare an offensive bw research program involving

botulinum toxin, clostridium toxin, and anthrax. Further investigations into Iraq's bw program will continue. The Persian Gulf War served to remind the coalition nations of the scale of impact of biological weapons and their broad strategic implications.

The World Today

The last few years have seen immense changes that few would have anticipated three years ago. The former Soviet Union and the Warsaw Pact have been dismantled. The bipolar situation of stability has shifted to one of increasing regional tensions. These changes of the last three years are continuing and few would be prepared to predict the outcome of the next three.

The Chemical Weapons Convention, which bans the development, production, possession, and use of chemical weapons, has been agreed at the Conference on Disarmament in Geneva, and will open for signature in January 1993, with entry into force likely to follow in 1995 or so. The convention includes all non-living chemicals in quantities that are not consistent with peaceful and protective purposes and provides for a more intrusive verification regime than any previous global, multilateral arms control arrangement.

The Persian Gulf War reminded the coalition states of the strategic utility of biological warfare, which requires much smaller quantities and far less sophisticated delivery means than for chemical weapons. Biological weapons are indeed the poor man's nuclear bomb.

In addition, there is a risk that biological weapons could become in future the agents of choice because they are not only more effective and require much less sophisticated delivery means than chemical weapons but they are also easier to hide. The Third Review Conference of the BWC held in September 1991 reinforced the norm that the development and production of biological weapons was prohibited, elaborated seven extended and improved confidence-building measures (CBMs), and mandated an Ad Hoc Governmental Group of Experts to examine potential verification measures from a scientific and technical viewpoint. This group started work in spring 1992 at a meeting from March 30 to April 10; a second meeting took place in Geneva from November 23 to December 4. Thus far, a series of verification measures both off-site and on-site have been identified. At the second meeting, these identified measures were examined. Each measure was defined and its characteristics, capabilities, and limitations summarized to form the basis for evaluation at a third meeting on May 24 to June 4, 1993.

In addition, the UN Special Commission established under Security Council Resolution 687 and charged with the elimination of Iraq's weapons of mass destruction capability has carried out inspections of bw sites in Iraq and has also elaborated a compliance-monitoring regime that was approved by the UN in Security Council Resolution 715 and published in S/22871/REV 1, dated October 2, 1992. Although this compliance-monitoring regime is an intrusive and demanding one, it does at least provide a starting point from which to consider how to devise a verification regime for the BWC.

The Way Ahead

There is no doubt at all about the strategic utility of biological warfare. The advances of biotechnology extend the producibility of such agents as well as offering the prospect of genetic manipulation to produce modified agents. It is important, however, not to assume that genetic manipulation makes the problem too difficult to solve. The traditional biological warfare agents that were the subject of the UK and U.S. programs of World War II and the subsequent years underwent very extensive trials to provide the necessary evidence to determine whether the microbial organisms would remain viable once disseminated in a weapon system and exposed to the natural environment. Although genetically modified agents can be developed, it is quite another thing to assume that such agents would survive in the natural environment, in which most microbial organisms are exceedingly fragile.

The way ahead is clearly based on a web of deterrence comprising a number of elements. These include (1) effective protective measures that reduce the range of materials that

Figure 2
Verification Measures

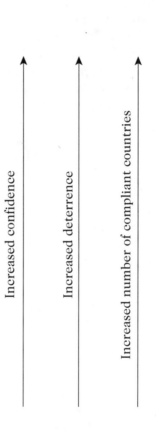

Political Declarations	BWCRC[a] II CBMs	BWCRC[a] III CBMs	Monitoring Patterns of Activity	Visits to High-Risk Sites	Anytime, Anywhere Inspections

Increased confidence

Increased deterrence

Increased number of compliant countries

[a] Biological and Toxin Weapons Convention Review Conference

can be used by an aggressor effectively and also reduce the military utility of biological warfare; (2) effective arms control agreements so that a potential aggressor cannot be certain that his program will not be found; (3) export monitoring and controls to increase the difficulties of acquiring biological warfare agents or the necessary technology for their production; and (4) a political commitment to react vigorously with a range of national and international responses—including the possibility of an armed response—if a state is found to be acquiring biological weapons or has gone so far as to use them.

The aim of any verification regime must be to deter a potential aggressor from seeking to acquire such weapons. Many nations will be deterred by the internationally binding commitment not to develop or acquire biological weapons. Such norms can be undermined, however, by the fact or fear of proliferation by potential aggressors. This in turn can encourage covert development of "retaliatory" capabilities. As the spread of the biosciences brings new biotechnology into areas of tension, so the risks to the BWC increase. The measures required to counter this threat are varied. Just as potential bw proliferators can be placed on a scale ranging from the international pariah bent on regional domination to the Western-oriented democracy concerned about its threatening neighbor, so there is a continuum of deterrent measures ranging from the rudimentary CBMs agreed at the BWC's Second Review Conference to an "anytime, anywhere" intrusive inspection regime (figure 2).

The shortcomings of the first CBMs for the BWC are well known. We also know that an intrusive inspection regime sufficient to deter the most determined violator would be generally unacceptable in terms of the risks to commercial and national secrets unrelated to biological weapons. Measures in between these extremes do not need to be 100 percent effective, provided there is indeed some probability of detecting noncompliance, in order to deter violation (figure 3). If we stop biological weapons going beyond the current 10 or so countries of concern, then we have achieved something, and the objective ought to be achievable without jeopardizing our

Figure 3

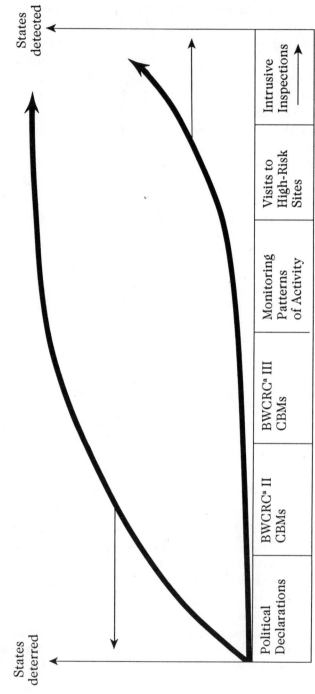

KEY POINTS
1. Intrusiveness of measures varies and increases from left to right.
2. Deterrence improves with increasing uncertainty about the ability to maintain a covert program.
3. Confidence in the ability of the regime to detect and deter cheating requires intrusiveness.

[a] Biological and Toxin Weapons Convention Review Conference

secrets, costing vast amounts of money, or creating false levels of confidence about the determined violators.

There is a cumulative benefit in locking nations into a compliance-monitoring regime. Over time, a web of deterrence can be created that will tighten to make life progressively more difficult for the established violator as well as deterring the new leader or victor in a coup who contemplates breaking out by turning his country's bioscience capabilities to illegal bw activity.

If a climate of international confidence can be made to develop through declarations and visits to the facilities of most concern, life for the determined proliferator will be tough: Should he stay outside such a regime and thus be under a cloud of mistrust, suffering, for example, from export controls, or should he endeavor to keep his efforts concealed within it? In these days of greater press freedom and information flow between scientists, the chances of keeping an illegal program totally under wraps are decreasing—the experience in Russia is a case in point.

The trilateral (UK-U.S.-Russian) agreement of September 1992 intended to boost confidence that the Russians will dismantle the former Soviet offensive bw program is beyond the scope of this discussion. Although it certainly constitutes a step forward, it is not intended to serve as a model of a water-tight verification regime.

A verification regime cannot be sharply defined as effective or ineffective in black or white but lies somewhere along a spectrum of effectiveness, with its position adjusted according to the costs and benefits arising from it.

Now that the CWC has been agreed and the UN Special Commission has demonstrated that a taut compliance-monitoring regime can be devised, there is a window of opportunity that we must all seize to seek to improve the BWC by the elaboration of a verification regime that is tailored to the smaller quantities and less sophisticated delivery means of biological weapons. It is all too easy to suggest that the task is too difficult and should therefore not be addressed. The threat to international and national security from the use of biological weapons by a potential aggressor is comparable to that of

nuclear weapons and cannot be ignored. We must all do whatever we can to ensure that biological weapons are effectively
and verifiably banned throughout the world.

3
The Proliferation of Biological Weapons
W. Seth Carus

This short essay examines three main issues: the extent of biological weapons (bw) proliferation; the motivations that lead countries to proliferate; and the implications of these developments for the United States. This review necessarily avoids specific discussion of countries known or suspected of possessing biological weapons, given that such information is not available on an unclassified basis. I will offer the following lines of argument. First, although the threat of biological warfare is not new, the extent of the problem is growing, both in the number of countries involved and the sophistication of what they might be able to do. Second, the entry costs and risks have been reduced by the dramatic advances in biotechnology over the past 20 years and by the increasing availability of dual-use, high-technology equipment. And, third, the potential threat poses a distinct military problem for the United States that has serious implications for the way in which the nation conducts both defensive and offensive operations.

The Extent of the Threat

What is the extent of the threat? For the past several years, U.S. government officials have noted that there are at least 10 countries known to have or suspected of having bw programs. This contrasts with the state of affairs in 1972 at the time of the signing of the Biological and Toxin Weapons Convention (BWC), when there were only four countries with bw programs.[1]

Although a number of countries have been identified as likely proliferators by U.S. government officials in the past, I will not attempt to identify those countries here. Instead, let me quote the congressional testimony of one intelligence analyst: "[S]ome of these nations are unfriendly to the U.S.;

some are located in the Middle East; and some are signatories to the Biological Weapons Convention."[2]

In addition to that comment, let me be specific about two particular points. First, the United States has a tendency to wish that the problem would go away because it seems too unsavory and too difficult to handle. Yet from a historical perspective the problem is not new. The United States has faced adversaries with offensive bw programs on several occasions in the past. German intelligence operatives reportedly attempted to infect horses and mules with anthrax and glanders during World War I. Indeed, the United States discovered that even prior to Germany's entry into that war, its agents were infecting animals being shipped to the Allies from U.S. ports. The laboratory to support these efforts was located in the Washington area at a private residence in Silver Spring. Whether these efforts had any effect is not clear from the historical record.[3]

During World War II, every major combatant had a bw program. Britain, Canada, and the United States all had large programs that are well known because declassified documents about them are available. In addition, Germany, Japan, and the Soviet Union also had programs, although they are not as well documented.[4]

Moreover, there are allegations that at least two countries employed biological weapons. German sources claim that Soviet guerrillas spread typhoid fever and typhus in occupied territory and that at least some Germans died as a result. Similarly, Japan reportedly used biological agents against the Chinese. These incidents were known in Washington and led to concern at the highest levels that Japan might employ such weapons against U.S. forces.[5]

By bringing up these examples, I do not mean to imply that the threat of biological weapons in 1917 or 1945 was as significant is it is today. Clearly that was not the case. It is worth noting, however, that the general problem, albeit in different form, has faced the United States through much of this century. And as the technology associated with biological warfare has improved, the threat has grown.

The biological revolution has made biological production processes increasingly central to economic well-being. Under such circumstances, sophisticated control over these processes has become more widespread and biological research and production technology is becoming as necessary to economic development as the traditional manufacturing industries. Moreover, the threat may not be limited solely to agents directed at humans, plants, or animals, but could include some agents intended for use against specific materials.

A second point that merits some elaboration is the specific threat that the United States faced during the Persian Gulf crisis. The coalition forces did not know the precise character of the bw threat posed by Iraq. As noted in the Pentagon's *Conduct of the War Report,* "In contrast to the reasonably comprehensive appreciation of Iraqi CW capabilities and doctrine, intelligence assessments of the BW threat were much more tenuous."[6] Nevertheless, it is believed that Iraq began large-scale production of biological agents in 1989 and that the Iraqis had a variety of delivery means at their disposal.

At the time of the war, the United States was seriously concerned that Iraq might be willing to use its arsenal of biological weapons. Accordingly, the problem of deterring their use became a key concern of U.S. policymakers during both Desert Shield and Desert Storm. These concerns are reflected in the *Conduct of the War Report,* which notes, "the inflamed rhetoric of Saddam Hussein implied a possible willingness to use such weapons to inflict mass casualties—perhaps to defeat the Coalition on the battlefield or perhaps to disrupt the will and cohesion of the Coalition."[7]

In the end, Iraq did not use biological weapons. Unfortunately, it is not known why. To once again quote from the *Conduct of the War Report:*

> It is not known why Iraq did not use chemical or biological weapons. It is not known what logistic preparations were made to enable such use should it have been ordered by Saddam. Nor is it known what specific actions by the U.S. and other members may have contributed to the Iraqi leader's decision not to use such capabilities. However, we

assume U.S. and other Coalition actions had a strong, restraining effect.[8]

These words speak for themselves. I would also add, however, that the coalition's escalatory capabilities almost certainly had a deterring effect on the Iraqis.

Motivations to Acquire

Why do countries seek to acquire bw capabilities? We have a relatively rich understanding of the motivations that lead proliferating countries to desire weapons of mass destruction. The perceived need for deterrence or compellence capabilities, a desire to influence the political-military calculations of potential adversaries, the search for national status, and even bureaucratic and personal factors can play a role in the initiation of such programs. From this perspective the interesting question is not why countries might seek weapons of mass destruction but rather why they would specifically choose to pursue biological weapons.

Unfortunately there is little hard data on this question because bw programs are generally not a matter for public discussion. Countries that are signatories to the 1972 Biological and Toxin Weapons Convention are prohibited from possessing or employing such weapons. Given the international norm that has developed against them, proliferating countries have strong incentives to keep secret their biological warfare–related activities.

There are at least a few exceptions to the lack of public. comment on bw programs that can provide some insight into the question of motivation. After the end of the Iran-Iraq War, in late 1988, a senior Iranian official was quoted in the Iranian press as describing chemical and biological weapons (cbw) as the "poor man's atom bomb," and arguing that his country needed such weapons to deter Iraq.[9] Given Iraqi use of chemical munitions against Iranian troops and Kurdish civilians, it is not surprising that an Iranian might come to hold such views.

In addition, even with the paucity of hard information, it is possible to identify four considerations that might make biological warfare programs attractive. First, as previously noted, biological weapons are viewed by the international community as weapons of mass destruction. Due to the challenges associated with development of other types of weapons of mass destruction, a country that feels a need for that type of capability could easily view a biological warfare program as the most cost-effective and lowest-risk solution to the requirement.

Second, virtually all the technology needed to support a bw program is dual use, obtainable off-the-shelf for a variety of legitimate purposes, and widely available. This dramatically reduces the complexity of pursuing such programs. The equipment to research, develop, and produce biological agents can be identical with that used in medical research. Production equipment need not differ from that used in a pharmaceutical industry. Even toxins have legitimate medical applications, and any country with an advanced medical industry has legitimate reasons for working on them. Indeed, much of the technology needed to weaponize biological agents is commercially available. For example, it is now possible to purchase remotely piloted vehicles equipped with sprayers for use in spreading pesticides.[10] Today, such systems are designed to spread biological agents intended to kill particular insect pests, but a dissemination system of this type might be easily adapted to military uses.

Third, detecting a clandestine biological warfare program is extremely difficult and thus the risks of being caught might be seen as relatively low. Because virtually all of the equipment associated with this kind of program can be used for legitimate purposes, it offers no easily discriminated, unambiguous signature. Moreover, existing international law permits defensive research, and in many instances the distinctions between prohibited and permitted activities are impossible to discern. Indeed, it is doubtful that even the most intrusive verification measure can provide definitive proof that a country has embarked upon an offensive bw program. And it is important to keep in mind that the costs of such measures— in terms of actual expense and potential for compromising vital proprietary information for industry—could be forbiddingly high.

Finally, proliferating countries may view a biological warfare program as an inexpensive route to acquisition of a weapon of mass destruction. Nuclear weapons programs are expensive, especially the efforts to acquire fissile material. Even chemical weapons (cw) programs are more expensive than commonly realized. Although small quantities of chemical agents can be produced relatively easily at low cost, to mass produce a chemical arsenal is not cheap. In contrast, it is far less expensive to develop biological warfare capabilities, although the total costs of fielding such capabilities may ultimately prove to be higher than anticipated. Several factors reduce the costs of such capabilities. So long as public health investments are made in the fight against disease, countries will acquire the basic technologies needed to work with biological agents. The ready availability of dual-use technology needed for legitimate public health purposes necessarily provides access to much of the paraphernalia needed to undertake nefarious activities.

There are additional factors that may make biological weapons more attractive than other weapons of mass destruction. Nuclear and chemical weapons programs are more detectable. Ironically, the verification provisions of the Chemical Weapons Convention (CWC) may accentuate this advantage by increasing the risks associated with a cw program, especially the danger that a clandestine program may be detected.

Implications for U.S. Security

What are the implications of the proliferation of biological weapons for U.S. security? Although this analysis emphasizes military considerations, this is not meant to denigrate the vital importance of efforts to inhibit or even roll back proliferation. Steps have been taken to address these issues in recent years, including approaches at the recent review conference of the BWC, the expansion of the role of the Australia Group, and the U.S. president's Enhanced Proliferation Control Initiative.

It is not enough, however, to view the problem as one of diplomacy and export control. As the Persian Gulf War indicated, it is also a military problem, with potentially serious ramifications for the conduct of strategy, combat operations, and coalition building. The Pentagon has concluded that the Gulf war experience indicates a need to do a better job of dealing with the problem. According to the *Conduct of the War Report*, "while the defensive capabilities of U.S. and other Coalition forces improved rapidly, CW/BW defensive readiness at the outset of the crisis was quite low."[11] In the future, the United States may not have six months to prepare its forces for conflict. Moreover, the report concludes that "BW defenses should be emphasized more fully in DOD programs. Inadequacies exist in detectors, vaccines, and protective equipment."[12]

The subject of defenses against biological weapons is beyond the purview of this essay, and in any case is discussed in detail in the chapter in this volume by David Huxsoll. There are two critical aspects of the issue, however, that relate directly to questions of deterrence. First, the perceived effectiveness of U.S. defenses is critical to the credibility of U.S. deterrence against use of biological weapons. Second, the United States may have to defend against organisms that are intended to attack matériel, crops, and livestock as well as people.

As the *Conduct of the War Report* makes clear, deterring Iraq from employing biological weapons was a matter of grave concern during the period leading up to the war. It is interesting to note that General Norman Schwartzkopf's recently published autobiography indicates that use of "unconventional" weapons (whatever they may be) was contemplated in the event Iraq resorted to biological warfare.[13]

In addition, the problems associated with attacks on biological warfare facilities also received considerable attention. There was serious concern that destruction of these facilities could lead to a widespread dispersal of biological agents. Accordingly, intensive efforts were made to minimize the danger through careful selection of time of attack and type of munitions employed.[14]

Conclusion

What should we conclude from this survey of proliferation? First, the problem is not a new one, but it is getting worse. Certainly, recent experience has given new urgency to U.S. efforts to respond to it. There is no reason to think that it will go away.

Second, the process of developing bw capabilities has been eased by advances in biotechnology and the widespread availability of dual-use equipment and materials that can be adapted for use in the development and production of biological weapons. The entry costs are extremely low when compared with other weapons of mass destruction.

Finally, the possession of biological weapons by a military adversary will have a direct impact on U.S. military operations, both defensively and offensively. The United States will need to protect its forces from possible bw attacks and also will have to undertake operations to destroy enemy research and development, production, and employment capabilities.

Note: The views expressed here are the author's personal views and not necessarily those of the Department of Defense.

Notes

1. Testimony of Dr. Barry J. Erlick, senior biological warfare analyst, U.S. Army, before the U.S. Senate Government Affairs Committee and the Permanent Subcommittee on Investigations, February 9, 1989.

2. Ibid.

3. This episode is discussed in Jules Witcover, *Sabotage at Long Tom: Imperial Germany's Secret War in America, 1914–1917* (Chapel Hill, N.C.: Algonquin Books of Chapel Hill, 1989), 93, 126–127, 136–137, 238.

4. Robert Harris and Jeremy Paxman, *A Higher Form of Killing: The Secret Story of Chemical and Biological Warfare* (New York: Hill and Wang, 1982).

5. Leo P. Brophy, Wyndham D. Miles, and Rexmond C. Cochrane, *The Chemical Warfare Service: From Laboratory to Field* (Washington, D.C.: Office of the Chief of Military History, 1959), 114; and Peter Williams and David Wallace, *Unit 731: Japan's Secret Biological Warfare in World War II* (New York: Free Press, 1989).

6. U.S. Department of Defense, *Conduct of the Persian Gulf War* (Washington, D.C., April 1992), 640.

7. Ibid., 639.

8. Ibid.

9. Hojjat o-Eslam Akbar Hashemi-Rafsanjani, then speaker of the Iranian Majlis, in Tehran IRNA (English), October 19, 1988, in Foreign Broadcast Information Service, *Daily Report, Near East and South Asia,* October 19, 1988, 55–56.

10. As an example of what is now commercially available, see *Aviation Week and Space Technology,* October 12, 1992, p. 17, which provides details of a Japanese remotely controlled helicopter intended for spraying pesticides and fertilizers.

11. *Conduct of the Persian Gulf War,* 640.

12. Ibid., 646.

13. H. Norman Schwartzkopf, *It Doesn't Take a Hero* (New York: Linda Grey, Bantam Books, 1992), 389–390.

14. *Conduct of the Persian Gulf War,* 154–155.

4
The Biotechnology Revolution and Its Potential Military Implications
Victor A. Utgoff

In the two decades since the United States abandoned its offensive biological warfare capabilities and the Biological and Toxin Weapons Convention (BWC) was created, there has been a revolution in the biological sciences and an entirely new form of technology for engineering biological organisms has appeared. This biotechnology offers three important new capabilities of interest to those concerned with the future of biological weapons (bw).

First, biotechnology provides a set of new tools that will promote an understanding, at the molecular level, of the structures and functions of the complex organic molecules that collectively make the human body and other forms of life work. Developing this kind of detailed understanding is very expensive and takes a long time, as the ongoing effort to map the human genome illustrates. Over time, however, biotechnology will make it possible to create an ever broader picture of the detailed functioning of the human body. Understanding will also improve of how chemical and biological agents can interfere with the proper functioning of the human body. This will lead to advances in medicine. Unhappily, it will also provide a detailed understanding of how to attack the human body better at the molecular level.

The development of chemical and biological agents will no longer be a matter of introducing agents into animals or even humans and observing their gross effects. Instead, by being able to understand precisely how particular biological agents interact with particular organic molecules in the body, and how those interactions interfere with the vital processes of life, scientists will be able to project how to alter these agents to make them even more efficient killers or incapacitants.

28

Second, biotechnology provides the tools with which to make the most delicate adjustments in the structures of organic molecules. Biological agents and toxins that are far more powerful than the most toxic of chemical agents are already known. Fortunately, most of them are currently impractical as weapons of war. In order to be practical in this role, a biological agent should be

- very toxic,
- fast acting,
- highly contagious,
- predictable in its effects,
- able to survive in air or water long enough to establish itself in the victim,
- not susceptible to the more common treatments that a doctor would naturally turn to,
- not readily destructible with the simpler water and air purification methods available, and
- susceptible to antidotes or prophylactics available to the attacker who uses it.

At least in theory, the ability to adjust the fine structures of complex organic molecules will allow agents that do not currently meet these criteria to be altered so that they do.

Third, biotechnology provides vastly more efficient and compact means for producing complex organic molecules. Production by these new methods requires fairly simple equipment. Examples are fermentors for growing cultures of bacteria into which the desired organic molecule has been introduced and centrifuges, strainers, and freeze dryers for concentrating and purifying the desired agents. For some types of agents, anthrax, for example, a room no larger than a garage can contain a production plant with sufficient capacity to create in a few weeks enough agent to destroy a dozen large cities.

Bioengineering production techniques also open the door to efficient mass production of antidotes to biological agents. Inability to mass produce antidotes has been one of the hurdles to creating practical biological weapons in the past.

These new capabilities presented by biotechnology create at least the theoretical possibility for new so-called designer biological weapons. They also permit the mass production of either new designer agents or, perhaps more worrisome, efficient and relatively low-cost mass production of agents that already exist in nature, such as anthrax spores or botulinal toxin. The obvious question is whether these new tools are being put to such uses.

Exploitation of Bioengineering

Elsewhere in this volume, Seth Carus has described how biological warfare programs appear to be proliferating around the world. But although there is strong evidence of the existence of a substantial number of national biological warfare programs, few observers have much insight into their precise nature. In some cases, biotechnology is suspected of being employed in the pursuit of new types of biological agents.

Certainly such efforts occurred in the former Soviet Union. As Russian president Boris Yeltsin has acknowledged, despite its BWC treaty commitment, the USSR had continued its efforts to develop an improved bw capability. The accidental release of anthrax spores in Sverdlovsk in April 1979 was one early hint. The apparent use of chemical and biological agents in Southeast Asia and Afghanistan, such as yellow rain and black rain, has never been satisfactorily explained and may indicate the development of altogether new biological agents.

There have been rumors that the Soviet Union was trying to create a virus that would multiply rapidly in the human body, create cobra venom as part of its biological makeup, and be extremely lethal as a result. And during 1989, Valentin Falin boasted that the USSR's answer to Star Wars might be a weapon developed with the aid of genetic engineering. Finally, although President Yeltsin's admission of Soviet noncompliance with the BWC was a positive step, the Russians have yet to explain what is going on in several institutes that are suspected of pursuing research in biological warfare.

Counterbalancing this rather speculative evidence of something new, the difficulties of developing wholly new agents are impressive. A practical agent has to have the variety of properties mentioned earlier. Creating one from the ground up appears to be a very complex task. Even the more likely path of modifying an existing agent to give it the characteristics needed to make it a practical weapon promises to be an expensive and complex undertaking.

Absent hard evidence that the former Soviet Union has somehow already succeeded, and noting that the enormous engine of natural evolution does not yield up dangerous new diseases like AIDS all that often, really dangerous *new* biological agents are probably some distance off. Moreover, even AIDS would be a very poor biological weapon. It is not easily transmitted and is far too slow in taking effect to be suitable as a weapon.

The problems do not end with the fact that creating new biological agents is very difficult. The ability of bioengineering technology to mass produce biological agents that already exist is a substantial new threat. Countries like Iraq are now able to put together dual-use, or even completely hidden, bioengineering plants that can create biological agents in large quantities. Mass production of such agents poses a serious threat, particularly because the countries in question can develop or buy dissemination systems that can be mounted on long-range aircraft or missiles.

Political-Military Implications of Biological Warfare

Suppose, then, that some renegade state is able to create a biological warfare capability that the United States is forced to take seriously. What might that mean? Let me offer a few speculations.

First, the combination of powerful biological agents with efficient dissemination systems mounted on long-range missiles or aircraft constitutes a very dangerous strategic threat to all population concentrations within range. An arsenal of such weapons could be a very powerful tool for intimidating neighboring states in peacetime or crises. It is theoretically possible that the proliferation of such weapons might have a stabilizing effect in regions where it takes place. If, on the other hand, deterrence broke down and such weapons were used, millions could die. In short, a biological arms race can pose risks to the Third World of much the same character as those posed to the participants in the East-West nuclear competition of the cold war.

Second, biological weapons deliverable with long-range missiles or aircraft could pose a very serious threat to U.S. or allied forces called on to intervene in defense of some vital regional interest that had been challenged by a bw-armed state. Interventions frequently require the introduction of masses of forces concentrated in a small area. Beachheads established by the Marines, airfields loaded with large numbers of aircraft, and divisions being assembled around an air- or seaport could be very lucrative targets for strikes with biological weapons.

Other possible uses of biological weapons can be imagined, such as use by terrorists, which is addressed by Robert Kupperman and David Smith elsewhere in this book. But the key question is what options might be available to the United States and its allies to ensure their continued ability to intervene in defense of important regional interests. Four broad approaches seem possible.

First, the United States can count on its ability to make devastating conventional or nuclear strikes in retaliation to deter the use of biological weapons against it. This solution is less than fully satisfactory for obvious reasons. The United States cannot be confident that the leadership of bw-armed renegade states will behave as rationally in the face of U.S. deterrent forces as it would like. Assuming that the United States is not going to create biological weapons itself, the devastation that may eventually be possible with these weapons may only be matched by nuclear weapons. Dependence on nuclear weapons to deter biological weapons works against longer-run U.S. interests in reducing the role of nuclear weapons.

Second, the United States could try to improve its defenses against bw attack. Passive defense measures, such as the use of protective masks and suits could be used. It could try to develop better antidotes for known biological agents. It could deploy theater missile defenses and air defenses to actively block bw attacks.

Given the high toxicity of bw agents and the correspondingly small size of biological weapons that can devastate cities,

the United States will also have to worry about how to stop
other less conventional means for making bw attacks. In sum,
defenses against bw attack will be important but costly and
unlikely to be perfect. It will also be a major problem to protect the populations of regional allies.

The United States could try to develop capabilities to make
effective disarming attacks against the biological warfare
capabilities of opponents, certainly as a precursor to intervening with otherwise vulnerable concentrations of conventional
military forces, and perhaps in other circumstances as well.
This will require extraordinary intelligence on the locations
and characteristics of an opponent's bw forces and facilities.

Destroying bw capabilities without killing large numbers of
innocent civilians may be a real problem in some cases. It may
take a long time to hunt down the opponent's bw capabilities,
in circumstances when time is short. It may be difficult to
know when and if their destruction is complete. In sum, developing the capability to destroy a renegade state's bw capabilities would be a real challenge and could prove impossible.

Finally, the United States could adjust its intervention
strategies and tactics to avoid giving the opponent particularly
lucrative concentrations of U.S. forces as targets. This might
mean using only long-range aircraft to strike the opponent
from beyond his reach. This too has its problems. It may be
impossible to achieve necessary U.S. military aims without a
ground campaign. The proliferation of bw capabilities could
thus force some fundamental changes in the ways the United
States can use military force to defend its overseas interests.

Conclusion

These arguments lead to the following conclusions. First,
biotechnology has changed the prospects for the creation of
practical biological weapons dramatically. Wholly new types of
biological weapons are going to be very difficult to create, but
this change opens up the potential for mass production of
biological agents that are already known and perhaps for some
alterations to improve upon them.

Second, there are signs that the Russians may have developed some new biological weapons. The United States should

press them harder to determine whether this is so and the nature of their discoveries. If they have discovered something new, it is important to understand its potential dangers to the world and to develop antidotes and other measures to neutralize it.

Third, if biological warfare capabilities proliferate unchecked, the United States may see very dangerous threats posed to its allies and the forces it might want to use overseas to defend its vital interests. The proliferation of biological warfare capabilities could mean some fundamental changes in the ways the United States considers using military forces to intervene overseas. In fact, absent some very good answers to the challenge posed by the proliferation of biological weapons, the United States could be forced to set a much higher threshold for such interventions.

Fourth, a variety of military measures exist by which to blunt the threat posed by such weapons, but they will be very difficult and expensive to create and are not likely to be fully satisfactory. Heading off the threat of biological weapons is less a military problem than a major political challenge.

Finally, some states will pursue bw capabilities for what they see as very legitimate deterrence and defense reasons. Eliminating their incentives to do so is likely to require credible assurances that their security is reliably provided for by other means. This will create pressures for the United States, regional security organizations, or the United Nations to underwrite the security of nations that might otherwise see the need for a bw-based strategic deterrent. Is the threat of proliferation of nuclear, biological, and chemical weapons strong enough to motivate Americans to accept the costs, risks, and political entanglements involved in providing reliable security assurances to a wide variety of additional nations?

Note: The views expressed here are solely the responsibility of the author.

5
Coping with Biological Terrorism
Robert H. Kupperman and
David M. Smith

To say that the United States is at a crossroads is simply to reiterate a truism that has become stale with repetition. But it has become increasingly less difficult to imagine a world in which the United States has lost its military capabilities to respond to new and unconventional threats from the next generation of international mavericks who will—make no mistake—follow in the footsteps of Qadhafi, Saddam Hussein, and Hafiz al-Asad. Americans are clearly in a different ball game, one that they ill understand.

On the security front, the United States is virtually unprepared to meet the kinds of threats most likely to occur. The greatest risk is that the nation will rest on the laurels of its Persian Gulf success. This is certainly not intended to detract from an extraordinary job of coordination, cooperation, and execution. Yet, in the final analysis, Desert Storm was a blip on the screen of regional conflict—an arena in which the United States has been slow to respond. In reality, the United States is not adequately prepared to cope with most kinds of attacks below the level of massive conventional warfare.

Terrorism—Saddam Hussein's second front—is one variation of potential threats. Throughout Desert Shield, and for much of Desert Storm, the specter of terrorism loomed large. Yet the threatened fusillade of terrorist events did not materialize. This is fortunate because the allies knew that Iraq planned devastating blows. It had the power to unleash the terrorists and it possessed the weapons, some of which were capable of inflicting mass destruction upon the members of the coalition.

Nevertheless, there were still nearly 200 attacks worldwide by terrorists sympathetic to Saddam. Most of them proved to be minor pinpricks, precisely because intelligence was shared in abundance. Today, U.S. defenses have been relaxed, difficulties in intelligence sharing have reemerged, and a note of apathy has crept back into counterterrorism activities. That makes the United States a vulnerable target.

Ironically, the threat may be much higher now than it was at the time of the war, given that it may take only months to plan, coordinate, and execute an effective terrorist attack. And the potential for impact is much greater. In the midst of war, terrorism is merely a sideshow. It is during the lulls that terrorism achieves center stage—precisely the effect the terrorists are after.

Terrorism is a high-leverage, low-risk form of warfare that has attracted many of the world's rogue leaders. President Ronald Reagan may have declared that terrorists "can run but they can't hide," but his statement proved in retrospect to be little more than hollow rhetoric. Syrian- and Iranian-sponsored terrorists blew a Pan Am jumbo jet and over 250 people out of the sky with total impunity (so far), also contributing, by the way, to the demise of Pan Am as a viable business. Pan Am 103 was attacked because it was an American symbol. There are many such symbols, dangerously vulnerable to attack, both around the globe and within the continental United States.

Clandestine attacks using chemical, biological, and radiological agents pose a significant risk and they may prove quite difficult to deter. These agents are inexpensive, readily obtainable, and largely unstoppable, except possibly by those nations that have prepared for such attacks by means of intelligence, detection, protective clothing, decontamination, vaccines, and emergency management. Clearly, the United States has not.

Some 20 nations are actively developing capabilities for using these agents. Responsible observers should ask themselves, To what end? Equally disturbing is the fact that these tools are filtering down to small nihilist groups operating abroad and in the United States. In 1988, a Japanese Red Army terrorist was caught on the New Jersey Turnpike with several bombs (although not of a chemical or biological nature). Recently, in Paris, a Red Army Faction (RAF) safe house (an apartment equipped with a primitive laboratory) was raided and found to have in it quantities of botulinal toxin, which is incredibly lethal. Last year, a plot by neo-Nazi "skin-heads" to pump hydrogen cyanide gas into a synagogue—a grisly reminder of World War II atrocities—was thwarted.

Games of regional power politics have outlasted the cold war, but technology is changing their reach and scope, with the result that new, real dangers are emerging. Small nations, even subnational terrorist groups, have the ability to inflict mass destruction upon their enemies. The means of delivery and the weapons have become ubiquitous. When Americans are faced with crisis, their tendency to panic and then to denial and apathy is their greatest danger. The aftermath of the Persian Gulf debacle is a case in point. Will the United States learn the right lessons? Or will it soon forget the more ominous clandestine threats?

Among all the terrible threats posed by Saddam Hussein during the Persian Gulf War, biological attack was by far the worst. Hundreds of thousands, conceivably millions, of people could have died in a well-executed urban attack. Had Saddam Hussein been slightly more clever, the United States and its coalition partners might have lost the war, their triumph wrenched from the jaws of victory by bolder tactics, including the use of biological agents against urban targets worldwide. The requisite technology, laboratory facilities, and aerosoliza-tion devices were already within the grasp of the weakest countries. The sad truth is that the United States, the world's sole surviving superpower, is still unprepared to cope with such a contingency.

The purpose of this paper is, first, to explore the physical threats posed by terrorists armed with live agents or toxins and, second, to evaluate the possible counters to these weap-ons, research and development (R&D) opportunities, emer-gency management, civil defense, and public education before and after a biological attack.

Threats

The use of biological agents as weapons dates back to antiq-uity. Over 2,000 years ago, Greeks and Romans used the corpses of victims of infectious diseases to contaminate their adversaries' wells. Since then, biological agents have been used repeatedly, for example, during the Crimean War, the British–American Indian conflicts, the Civil War, the Boer War, and probably in Southeast Asia. Advances in biological weaponry have paralleled military developments of conventional and even nuclear arms, especially when the progress in genetic engineering is considered. Fortunately, because of the moral abhorrence felt by the West over the use of these insidious weapons, they were not used during either World War I or World War II. Even with these beliefs, however, had World War II not ended when it did, biological weapons would undoubtedly have been used. Five thousand anthrax-laden cluster bombs were in production in the United States, destined for Berlin. When the war ended, production ceased and the bombs were destroyed.

Advances in medical care, health research, agriculture, pharmacology, and biotechnology, especially recombinant DNA technology, while dramatically enhancing human lives, have also introduced new tools for warfare. The same equipment and technologies used to save lives can be readily directed toward the production and effective use of biological weapons. Because of these advances, biotechnology equipment and expertise have been widely disseminated throughout industrialized and many Third World nations. Moreover, U.S., European, and Asian universities graduate literally thousands of scientists and engineers each year with the technical acumen needed to produce and effectively use biological weapons.

Although cutting-edge biotechnology research requires an infrastructure of sophisticated equipment and laboratories, many of the more effective biological agents can be produced in sufficient quantities for terrorist use by relatively primitive means. Virtually any infectious microorganism or metabolic product of an organism that elicits incapacitating or lethal effects in plants, animals, or humans has potential utility as a biological weapon. Even today, the most effective and easy-to-use agents occur naturally in the environment and are not man-made (i.e., genetically engineered).

Biological agents (live pathogens and toxins) are commonplace—and some of them are all too effective. Because they are found in abundance, easily grown, and lethal in minute quantities, three agents stand out as prototypical.

Anthrax (*Bacillus anthracis*), botulinal toxin, and the plant toxin ricin are prototypical biologicals. Seed cultures of anthrax are readily obtained; they are found in the soil of cattle country or at times in sheep's wool. *B. anthracis* is endemic to large areas of the world, including Iraq.

Anthrax is grown aerobically, a luxuriant product of fermentation, much the way beer is brewed. But the similarity ends here, for when inhaled anthrax spores kill with virtual certainty. The mean lethal inhalatory dosage is 10^{-8} gm, or, in principle, were the spores distributed appropriately, one gram would be enough to kill more than one-third of the population of the United States. Fortunately, such an attack is not feasible. But a single, simpler attack, executed by individuals of limited technical competence, could kill hundreds of thousands. This was demonstrated by the United States Army when, in the 1950s, it dispersed live, nonpathogenic agents in the New York City subway system in order to test the utility and ease of execution of an anthrax attack.

B. anthracis (anthrax) is endemic and enzootic in many parts of the world; some strains are highly virulent and can cause death within 24 hours after being inhaled or ingested. Death results from pneumonia, systemic infection (septicemia), and subsequent organ failure. As noted earlier, it is quite easy to culture in a laboratory. Preparing it for dissemination as spores requires some expertise, but the terrorist can practice disseminating bacillus species that are not pathogenic to humans. For example, *B. thuringiensis,* which is used to control caterpillars, can be used safely to simulate anthrax.

Botulinal toxin is an exotoxin that causes paralysis by blocking the transmission of nerve impulses at neuromuscular or neuroglandular junctions, resulting in congestion and hemorrhage in all the organs and especially in the central nervous system. Death usually occurs within 24 to 48 hours.

Botulinal toxin is produced by *Botulinum clostridium,* a bacterium found virtually everywhere. When food, such as canned salmon, is improperly handled, botulinal poisoning may occur. The Type-A toxin, when crystallized, has a mean lethal ingestive dose of a microgram, making it the most lethal substance known. Unfortunately, it is also easily produced and is readily dispensable.

Ricin is obtained from the castor bean. The toxin is insidious. When inhaled, less than a milligram causes death, often within hours. All that is needed is the castor bean and an adventuresome terrorist willing to extract the toxin from it. The solvent extraction of the protein albuminoid toxin is a well-documented, trivial, two-step procedure.

Ricin is a cytotoxin with a predilection for the hemovascular system. Death usually occurs from pulmonary edema and circulatory collapse. For quite some time, ricin was the suspected culprit in Legionnaires' disease. It was the agent in the Bulgarian umbrella killings. During World War II and the 1950s, ricin was stockpiled by the ton.

Anthrax, *Botulinum clostridium,* and ricin were among Saddam Hussein's selected instruments. Most of Iraq's clandestine biological facilities may still exist, despite the efforts to eliminate them. Syria, Iran, Libya, North Korea, and Cuba have also chosen these agents.

Although there are more sophisticated agents, the three listed above are superb model agents because of their high toxicities and relative ease of production. Once terrorists have made sufficient quantities of their agent of choice, they have to develop a delivery system, which, not surprisingly, presents no difficulties because commercial units for aerosolizing liquid and solid materials are readily available.

The most effective means of delivering toxic agents to large populations is via aerosol clouds, with the toxic particles or droplets being highly respirable. Respirable particles have mean aerodynamic diameters of 1 to 3 microns. (Aerodynamic diameter results from the particle's physical size, shape, and density.) Respirable particles are readily inhaled and deposited in the peripheral portions of the lungs, where they are readily absorbed if soluble in biological fluids. Many chemicals are absorbed and distributed systemically almost as fast as when they are injected intravenously. They also remain suspended in air for extremely long periods. A rule of thumb is that respirable particles settle at only 2 to 3 centimeters per hour.

Wind and sunlight are the principal means of inactivating biological agents once they have been dispersed.

Even if less than optimal aerosol delivery systems that generate particles larger than respirable sizes are used, it is probable that these particles would remain suspended in the atmosphere for a long enough period to infect large numbers of people.

Obtaining starting cultures for anthrax and *Botulinum clostridium* is easily accomplished because these micro-organisms are found in most areas of the world and are widely studied. Although distribution of these organisms is now monitored by the U.S. Federal Bureau of Investigation and the law enforcement agencies of other governments, culture samples can be obtained under the guise of use in legitimate medical research. Once reference samples are obtained, they can be put into production for terrorist activities. If a terrorist group decides not to use reference samples, it can readily isolate and grow the organisms from areas where they are endemic or enzootic.

Aerosol dispersal technology is easy to obtain from open literature and commercial sources, and equipment to aerosolize biological agents is available as virtually off-the-shelf systems produced for legitimate industrial, medical, and agricultural applications. With access to a standard machine shop, it would not be difficult to fabricate aerosol generators and integrate components to produce reliable systems for dispersing micro-organisms or toxins.

Illustrative Scenarios

Although the circumstances under which biological agents can be employed as terrorist weapons seem limitless, we offer three scenarios to illustrate the effectiveness of such weapons:

1. The date is late spring 1993 and internal violence in the former USSR has erupted into virtual civil war. Hopes for peace in the Middle East have been dashed. Iraq, now emboldened by Russian and Ukrainian hard-liners, retains ruthless elements of the Abu Nidal organization to commit a monstrous act against Israel and the United States and leave

no signature. New York City is the target, the financial center of the world and home to millions of Jewish-Americans. Saddam Hussein will get even; the United States will never be the same. The plot is doable and plausibly desirable. A fishing vessel sails around Manhattan Island, starting at the entrance to the East River. To avoid suspicion, the vessel has the external trappings of a commercial boat normally present in these waters. At a speed of three knots up the river, an airborne cloud of mono-dispersed respirable anthrax spores, suspended in a suitable medium (e.g., propylene glycol or an inert powder), would be released from the nozzles of an aerosol generator. The release point would be 35 feet above the waterline and the anthrax spores would be released at a rate of 2 kilograms per hour (2×10^{11} lethal dosages per hour). A grayish, overcast day is chosen, so that the advantages of a stable atmosphere are obtained. By conservative estimate, more than 400,000 people die within 48 hours. Manhattan and its surroundings are contaminated and may have to be evacuated. After the attack, the fishing vessel heads to the open sea, where it is destroyed. The United States must respond, but against whom and how?

2. In late 1993, Germany's RAF terrorist group strikes with a vengeance in the United States. Ten milligrams of botulinal toxin (10^5 lethal doses) are injected into bulk milk in a commercial processing plant, after it has been pasteurized. Each carton of milk or subsequent portion of a dairy product like ice cream contains thousands of fatal doses. The target plant is a supplier to a vender serving the Senate dining room. When the toxin takes effect, the victims experience crippling nausea, vomiting, cramps, double vision, and muscular paralysis. Casualties number 2,000 to 4,000 with at least 50 percent of them dying.

3. The Animal Liberation Front places a small nitrogen-pressurized aerosol generator in an air vent of the ballroom of a major Washington, D.C., hotel housing the annual meeting of the American Academy of Arts and Sciences. Five kilograms of ricin are dispersed over three hours. Two thousand people are exposed. Within hours after the dinner, 11 people collapse. By morning, 170 people are critically ill or dead. A medical emer-

gency is declared and panic ensues. Federal and local health and law enforcement personnel are mobilized. That morning, the aerosol device is discovered. Within hours, ricin is reported to be the agent. An act of biological terrorism has been documented, an ugly vignette reminiscent of the Legionnaires' disease outbreak of some 15 years ago.

In the event of the anthrax attack described above, New York City, if not the entire United States, would "stop" for months, its infrastructure and health resources overwhelmed. Fear of contamination, which would cloister most New Yorkers initially, would give way to the pragmatics of survival (food and water). Martial law would likely follow because the city would be gridlocked, its people frantic. The rats, which already outnumber the human population, would be well on the way to a permanent victory. If the attack were extensive, large portions of the city might be abandoned, even condemned by whatever city government remains. New York City would be as deserted as Hamburg in 1943, but eerily the buildings would still be standing.

If only for purposes of revenge and national distraction, U.S. intelligence and law enforcement agencies would ferret out the culprits. Once the sponsoring state is found, the United States would face the ultimate dilemma of whether to attack a country that may well have nuclear weapons.

Resolving the Problem

Resolving the terrorist problem requires vigilance by the United States, something history shows to be difficult for this country and made even less possible by the trivializing effect of television. Even if the United States acts today, it may be unprepared for years to cope with the primary emergency, even as it retains the capacity to thwart a limited nuclear attack. The U.S. government will have been ensnared by inattention to the changing modes of warfare and an inflexibility brought on by decades of cold war.

To improve its protective posture, the United States should pursue an all-embracing concept that includes proactive intelligence collection, the will and the weaponry to destroy the biological arsenal of a Saddam Hussein, the technological ability to destroy clouds of pathogens, countermeasures such as lasers or bleach-saturated "counterclouds," protective measures (civil defense and public education), and command post and field simulations intended to develop realistic recovery plans. The Federal Emergency Management Agency should lead this effort. The White House should prepare an emergency management protocol to safeguard U.S. national resources. The objective would be to have a plan in place to recover from a massively destructive biological attack on the United States without additional self-inflicted wounds.

A central element of this effort should be creation of a chemical and biological counterpart to the Nuclear Emergency Search Teams (NEST). NEST was formed in the mid-1970s to meet evolving command and control, technical, behavioral, law enforcement, search, disarmament, and decontamination needs, after a number of episodes demonstrated the need to assess nuclear weapon extortions, to locate improvised or stolen atomic weapons rapidly, and to deactivate them. Fortunately, the more than 100 nuclear extortions to date have all been hoaxes, and no atomic bombs have been found. Nevertheless, the team(s) has performed admirably both in Europe and in the United States. Numerous exercises involving "stolen" nuclear devices have been held, and a well-honed ability to assess and cope with nuclear threats has emerged.

No such capability exists for chemical and biological threats. We propose formation of a chemical/biological analog, CBEST. This is not another mere bureaucratic invention. Parallel to advances in detection and countermeasures, an interdisciplinary capability must be forged to cope with the threat and consequences of biological attack. Anything less would be irresponsible. It may take as much as a decade for Saddam Hussein to fabricate a nuclear weapon, but only a few months would be needed to deliver an anthrax cloud over a U.S., European, or Middle Eastern city. Staffing and equipping CBEST would be a relatively inexpensive and sane response to the proliferation of biological weapons to states known to sponsor terrorism and to those that might see ideological virtue in humbling the world's sole remaining superpower.

The U.S. Department of Energy relied upon the national laboratories for help in framing the NEST concept and for bringing it to life. Now again the Los Alamos National Laboratory and its sister laboratories can develop the detection and countermeasure technologies needed to cope with biological warfare. Moreover, the laboratories can construct simulations that predict cloud movement, horizontal and vertical dilution, and residual virulence. Using meteorological data, active defenses, such as high-power ultraviolet (UV) lasers and "countercloud missiles," can be deployed, and passive measures, such as evacuation, might be prepared as well.

Conclusion

The use of biological agents as weapons of terrorism, insurgency, or war—no matter how repugnant—cannot be excluded. Indeed, its likelihood is probably increasing, as biological weapons proliferate and the stability of the cold war balance of power passes. The potential was demonstrated during the Persian Gulf episode, when there was every reason to fear SCUD attacks dispersing anthrax over Israel and killing tens of thousands. Nor is the United States immune from such attacks.

Reasonable preparedness measures should be taken now. Among these are technological innovations designed to detect and identify pathogens and toxins; active defenses (counterclouds of disinfectants and high-power UV lasers); pharmacological defenses (vaccines, toxoids, monoclonal antibodies, and antibiotics); disinfectant aerosols built into air-conditioning systems of large buildings; and effective decontaminants following an attack. Less exotic forms of protection should be a priority as well. Development and testing of advanced protective garb for those engaged in cleanup should be undertaken. Low-technology approaches also deserve attention, such as taping door rims and using vacuum cleaners in homes to create a positive pressure relative to the outside, all as part of a comprehensive, intelligent civil defense program. Beyond technological development, an emergency operations, command and control, and training apparatus should be carefully designed and implemented. CBEST, the analog of the successful NEST team, should be constructed and undergo exercises regularly.

Biological warfare is frightening. But pretending that the threat does not exist will only lead to needless injury, death, and public hysteria because reasonable protective measures will not have received sufficient attention.

6
Arms Control Programs and Biological Weapons
Michael Moodie

As noted in earlier chapters, the approach of the United States to the problem of biological warfare has for decades reflected a balance of political, military, and diplomatic policies, the purposes of which are to make as unlikely as possible biological attack on the United States, its allies, or their military forces, to diminish the casualties if such attack occurs, and to prevent the spread of such heinous weapons. This chapter focuses on arms control and the contribution it makes and can make in the future to achieving these goals, but it must be remembered that arms control cannot be considered in isolation from the larger policy framework. Considerations about what is feasible and desirable in the nature of revisions to arms control approaches must be shaped by a careful reading of the promise and limits of other policy approaches, including biological defense programs, export controls, active diplomacy, and other legal instruments.

The centerpiece of the arms control approach in the biological area is, of course, the Biological and Toxin Weapons Convention (BWC). This multilateral treaty was negotiated in 1970 and 1971 after the United States unilaterally renounced its possession of biological weapons (bw). It also reflected a willingness of the international community at that time to separate the biological problem from the chemical one, and to seek first a biological weapons ban because agreement there seemed much easier to achieve than in the chemical area. The BWC was opened for signature on April 10, 1972, and entered into force on March 26, 1975. There have subsequently been three conferences to review its performance and possible measures to strengthen the regime, in 1979, 1986, and 1991. Compliance concerns have given special impetus to these reviews, starting with the Sverdlovsk incident at the first session and going on to the shadow cast by the Iraqi biological program and the larger proliferation problem at the most recent. The treaty designates the United Nations (UN) and specifically the Security Council as the vehicle for resolving doubts about compliance but provides no inspection or monitoring provisions to support this task. Hence much of the debate at the review conferences has focused on measures to strengthen confidence that states are complying with their commitments. There has also been increased attention to more effective compliance mechanisms where malefactors are at work. The convention stands as the basic international norm against bw proliferation, and it now commands the support of almost 120 nations.

The September 1991 Review Conference

The Third Review Conference in September 1991 reflected the current state of the regime and thinking about it within the international community. Thus the discussion there provides a useful framework for examining the key issues confronting arms control practitioners attempting to come to grips with the menace of biological weapons.

From the U.S. perspective, the review conference was very positive. One reason was the cooperative spirit that the states parties to the convention brought to the exercise. Gone was the traditional posturing and antisuperpower rhetoric that was so common in previous review conferences. The experience with Iraq and the Persian Gulf War transformed the bw threat from a theoretical possibility into a tangible security concern for many states, which translated into a positive attitude toward the work of the conference and a good deal of progress. The result was a strengthened convention.

The United States was also very pleased that the review conference bolstered the BWC as the critical international norm against bw proliferation. This was an important outcome for the Bush administration, which has emphasized the strengthening of such norms as a major strand in its approach to nonproliferation problems across the board. It has tried to achieve this by means of concluding the Chemical Weapons Convention (CWC) while also reinforcing and strengthening the regimes embodied in the Nuclear Non-Proliferation Treaty (NPT) and the BWC.

Another very positive outcome was the fact that serious work on problems with the BWC had an educative effect among states parties to the convention. Because the BWC generally receives only episodic attention from senior policymakers among states parties, a tendency has emerged to seek quick fixes to problems as they assume sudden political prominence because of an international gathering or event. Such fixes come to be debated virtually without reference to the experience of the international community in trying to cope with these problems or to the necessity of integrating political, technical, and military factors. Nor are they always debated by those with an adequate scientific base on which to make wise political judgments. The Third Review Conference helped to focus attention on these factors, and left many of those charged with stewardship of this treaty with the hope that coming years may bring real fixes rather than mere Band-Aids to the problems confronting the regime.

A brief issue-by-issue review illustrates this basic line of argument.

Assistance. Two separate issues related to assistance are identified in the BWC. One relates to the assistance rendered to states subject to biological attack, for which there is a general but vague commitment in the treaty text. The Third Review Conference reinforced the commitment of the states parties to consult on allegations of use when they are made by any state party and to cooperate fully with investigations by the UN secretary general, who is authorized to explore such allegations if asked to do so. The conference stressed that in the case of alleged use, the UN is called upon to take appropriate measures that could include a request to the Security Council to consider action in accordance with the UN Charter. "Sanctions" was a dirty word during the conference, but the option to pursue sanctions in the event of use exists.

The second assistance issue relates to the peaceful use of biological research and biotechnology and to technological assistance among states parties for this purpose. Many developing countries made this area their top priority for the Third

Review Conference. In most cases, however, their proposals went well beyond what developed nations could accept because of their insistence on the most extreme, automatic, and wide-ranging forms of biotechnology transfer. The developed world views with some unease the increasing access of states with ambitious military plans or programs to advanced dual-use technologies, especially given growing fear about the proliferation of biological weapons. The West also doubted the virtue of the automaticity of the assistance desired by the nonaligned, who seemed to be looking for not just assistance but wholesale industrial development. Thus the language on assistance of the final declaration was kept consistent with the general thrust of the treaty itself, and no new specific commitments appear there.

Confidence-building measures. Perhaps the single most positive outcome of the Third Review Conference was the package of confidence-building measures (CBMs) agreed upon by the states parties. The basic approach to strengthening the BWC adopted in earlier review conferences and thus made a continued top priority by the United States emphasizes openness and transparency as the best way to generate the requisite confidence that states are in compliance with the agreement. Openness and transparency, therefore, became major elements of the U.S. approach and were encapsulated in the CBMs that it and others proposed.

The final package of CBMs included the strengthening of four CBMs agreed at the 1986 Review Conference as well as the addition of several new ones. Of special importance to the United States was the measure requiring the exchange of information on national biological defense programs. This measure asks a state party to provide information about its work on biological defense; specifically, it asks for a general declaration about whether it conducts such work as well as specific information about the program, such as funding levels, facilities where the activities occurred, program organization, and so on. In essence, the United States was asking other states parties to provide the kinds of information that the United States already provides on an open basis to the Congress and elsewhere.

The other CBMs from the earlier review conference that were reaffirmed or modified include the provision of information on outbreaks of infectious diseases to the World Health Organization, the encouragement of the publication of results of research on biology and biotechnology, and the active promotion of contacts among scientists in the international community working in similar areas.

The new CBMs included an agreement to add a "null declaration." The purpose of such a declaration is to induce states with no relevant biological activities to participate in the confidence-building process by getting them to report something, even if only that they are not doing anything. More important was agreement on a declaration of past offensive and defensive research and development programs. Finally, a measure was also approved for the declaration of facilities, both governmental and nongovernmental, producing vaccines licensed by the state for the protection of human beings. The measure upset industry representatives when U.S. participants returned from Geneva and met with them to report on the outcome of the conference. Their concern is with public relations: they are worried that because their activities must be declared under this CBM, they will be branded in the public mind as in some way associated with biological weapons despite the fact that their activities are perfectly innocent. This is not an overwhelming obstacle, but it reflects the degree of sensitivity associated with the bw problem.

Soviet/Russian compliance. The United States and the United Kingdom highlighted in their plenary presentation their determination that the Soviet Union (then three months from extinction) had not complied with its BWC obligations. The Third Review Conference's final declaration included a strong statement of concern about noncompliance and about continuing compliance doubts. The declaration also noted that these continuing doubts and the problems of noncompliance would undermine both the convention itself and arms control in general.

The Soviet representatives argued that the compliance issue had to do with "misunderstanding," insisting that U.S. concerns about compliance arose out of ambiguities in the text of the convention. Thus they pressed for language that would provide what they called a more precise understanding of what exactly is permitted and prohibited under the convention which, they argued, would convince the United States and all other doubters that the Soviet Union was in fact fully compliant with the treaty.

Even prior to the conference, as well as subsequently, the United States and the United Kingdom had been working with the government of the Soviet Union and later Russia to resolve their concerns with compliance. President Boris Yeltsin's acknowledgment in early 1992 that the charges about noncompliance were correct was welcomed as a very positive first step. His claim was reaffirmed in the Russian declaration provided as part of the new CBM on past offensive and defensive programs. U.S. officials were grateful to have their charges vindicated, not just because it was some compensation for the abuse heaped on them at various times during the 1980s for making such charges, but also because it meant that the compliance problem in Russia may begin to be resolved and the BWC set free of this fundamental problem.

Yeltsin's March 1992 acknowledgment that the Soviet Union had indeed violated the BWC by pursuing an offensive program was followed in April by a decree outlawing activities prohibited by the BWC. Since that time the United States and the United Kingdom have followed up in a series of discussions with the Russians that led to the September 1992 joint statement, which will permit some ad hoc visits among the three parties as a way to begin to define the extent of the Soviet bw program and to investigate suspect sites. Over the long term this agreement should—it is hoped—put compliance concerns to rest. Thus it must be understood as an exercise in compliance broadly conceived rather than verification narrowly defined. This is an effort designed specifically to generate confidence that Russia is now fully compliant with the BWC and that noncompliant activities have been terminated.

Verification. The verification issue became the most contentious issue and proved to be the last one resolved at the Third Review Conference. The absence of a detailed verification regime was often noted in the preparatory work for the conference, and many states felt that with the CWC apparently reaching conclusion on a verification package and the general improvement in verification techniques since the BWC was written, the time was approaching to add a verification package—perhaps more or less directly from the chemical talks. Indeed, at the conference, the majority of states parties argued that the BWC could be strengthened by the addition of even a weak verification regime because of its promise in deterring cheating. The United States shares the international desire for stronger verification and compliance mechanisms, but its reading of the possibilities is rather different. In a conclusion informed by a careful review of experience gained in the chemical, nuclear, and conventional areas, and of the technical aspects of militarily significant, offensive biological warfare programs, the United States argued that the BWC was not effectively verifiable and that it had not identified any way to make it so. Put simplistically, the argument was between those who argued that "some verification is better than none" and the United States, which contended that "bad verification was worse than none."

The United States did not close the door entirely on new approaches that may become possible because of changing international political circumstances or technologies, so a continuing discussion of verification issues in anticipation of the Fourth Review Conference was planned. The United States argued that a distinction must be made between political judgments about the benefits and costs of different verification measures and the scientific and technical judgments associated with potential verification activities—and that political judgments can be made only with a sophisticated understanding of the scientific and technical base, something not widely in evidence among the diplomats attending the Third Review Conference.

Thus an experts group on verification was created. Its mandate is narrowly defined: to evaluate proposed verification measures from a scientific and technical standpoint. The group has met several times under the chairmanship of Ambassador Tibor Toth of Hungary. A list of 21 measures has been proposed, covering both off-site and on-site activities. Each of these measures is to be evaluated in terms of six criteria set forth in the final declaration of the Third Review Conference. These are a measure's strengths and weaknesses; its ability to differentiate between prohibited and nonprohibited activities; its ability to resolve ambiguities about activities; the technology, manpower, and equipment it requires; its financial, legal, and safety implications; and finally its impact on scientific research, cooperation, industrial development, and protection of proprietary information.

The continuing debate about BWC verification has reflected quite different ideas about what verification means. For some it appears to run the complete range from measures that have a largely political content, including declarations and CBMs, to highly intrusive inspections that would entail on-site visits "anywhere, anytime." The United States agrees that some of these various measures can and do make some contribution to strengthening the regime, but confidence-building does not constitute verification and should not be subsumed by a definition of verification. They are distinctly different activities, the effectiveness of which must be evaluated by different criteria.

Part of the ongoing debate arises from the distinction between deterrence and detection. A measure must have some ability to detect noncompliant activities if it is to be genuine verification. Many of the activities mentioned above can contribute to deterrence, but their deterrence effect will be reliable only if there is a credible prospect of detection. Only if a state thinks it might get caught cheating, and will pay a price for being caught, will it be deterred. Verification measures are important to arms control treaties because they deal with the problems of *noncompliance.* This is why the United States would take issue with those who argue that the emphasis in verification should be on demonstration of compliance. Iraq, after all, demonstrated to the satisfaction of the International Atomic Energy Agency that it was in compliance with the NPT. Demonstrating compliance is, therefore, not enough. The risk of detection must exist to a significant degree, and, from the perspective of the United States, the case has not yet been made that, given their costs and benefits, any of the various inspection concepts would credibly be seen by a determined proliferator as a barrier to a surreptitious bw program because of the reasonable likelihood that such inspections would detect the relevant research, development, and production activities or distinguish them from activities that could be defended as legitimate.

Thus, these two problems—mistaking detection for deterrence and the difference and confusion over the purposes of verification—are at the heart of the U.S. concern about the current debate within the international community about verification of the BWC.

National measures. The BWC also provides a framework within which states parties can undertake unilateral measures to strengthen the regime. This short review of the arms control approaches to the bw problem will conclude with a discussion of two legal approaches currently being pursued at the national level in support of the goal of ridding the world of biological weapons.

One aspect is domestic legislation. The United States sought language in the final declaration that would commit states parties to enact legislation that would facilitate enactment of the convention, including laws criminalizing involvement in bw activities of an offensive rather than a defensive character. This is something the United States has already done itself. Although the final declaration did not endorse the U.S. proposal, the conference did acknowledge that legislation to facilitate enactment of the convention might include penal legislation. It was also agreed to consider extraterritorial application of legislation when such practice is consistent with a state's national constitution.

The other aspect relates to export controls. The inclusion in the final declaration of a specific reference to export controls in a way that would have committed states to such controls was not acceptable to all states, especially to the non-aligned nations. Nevertheless, the final declaration did reaffirm the reference in the convention to controlling the transfer of prohibited items to any recipient, rather than a narrower prohibition on transfers favored by some, which would have recognized the right to control such transfers only to nonparties.

Export controls in the biological area began in earnest in 1989, at which time the United States was one of the few countries with export controls on microorganisms related to toxicity. In late 1989, the Australia Group, created to share information about chemical weapons proliferation and to coordinate export control policies among key Western countries, began to exchange information related to biological weapons at the end of its meetings. This exchange of information allowed for the development by the group of what it called "warning guidelines," which were given to academia, industry, and other relevant audiences in order to prevent the inadvertent transfer of a potential bw-related technology or capability to a suspect state.

At the same time, the United States began to transform its export controls because, up until that point, everything not on the list was controlled. There was a strong sense, however, that if multilateral export controls were to be effective, positive controls, that is, controls on things that were specified and agreed, had to be developed. As a result, the United States began to change its approach toward development of such a positive list.

Prior to the Persian Gulf War, interest was growing within the international community about export controls, but the war greatly strengthened that interest. By the time of the Third Review Conference in September 1991, the Australia Group was discussing technically what should be controlled. The information-exchange portion of Australia Group meetings was transformed from a 30-minute exercise to perhaps half a day.

At the moment, there are four lists that have been discussed by the Australia Group addressing human pathogens, plant pathogens, animal pathogens, and dual-use equipment. The human pathogens list has basically been agreed, and it has been adopted and promulgated by the U.S. Department of Commerce. There is disagreement, however, on the plants and animals lists. The differences center on whether the elements on the list should be subject to export controls or just constitute an industry awareness guideline. With respect to the last list, on dual-use equipment, it is likely that there will be some fine tuning, but this list should be approved at the Australia

Group meeting in December 1992. [Editor's note: such a list was so approved.]

Beyond the Bush Administration

At the time this is written, the newly elected administration of Bill Clinton is assembling its team and conducting major policy reviews. The president-elect and his appointees will assume responsibility for stewardship of the BWC, not just because of the formal duties of the United States as one of the three depositaries (together with the United Kingdom and Russia) but because of the U.S. stake in preventing the spread and use of biological weapons and the central challenges of leadership awaiting it in this area.

The Clinton administration will no doubt define its own policies and approaches to bw arms control. It may decide to pursue verification measures more aggressively. But it may not. There will be sources of continuity as well as sources of change in U.S. policy, however. The U.S. commitment to the BWC transcends the views of any one administration, and its ideas about how to work to strengthen the regime are firmly rooted in its 20-year history and the extensive experience of the United States in building and working with arms control measures. Looking to the future, arms control can and will make a strong contribution to ameliorating the problem of biological weapons. Its contribution will be diminished if a clumsily designed inspection system is added to the regime that over time serves to encourage proliferators, weaken resolve among states parties to deal with the political aspects of compliance, and erodes confidence in the regime. But there is a real and continuing challenge to strengthen the regime, to work with agreed measures, and to recraft and refine as necessity warrants in the years ahead.

7
The U.S. Biological Defense Research Program
David L. Huxsoll

The Biological Defense Research Program is the vehicle by which the United States conducts research, development, testing, and evaluation (RDT&E) of defensive measures and matériel with which to meet threats of biological warfare. Although the program has existed for a number of years, it still faces challenges, among them the need for new and improved medical defenses, detection and warning capabilities, physical protection—both individual and collective—and methodologies for direct neutralization of all forms of potential biological threats. The maintenance of a sophisticated biological defense technology base gives the United States the capability to respond to unexpected threats and to prevent a technological surprise.

The proliferation of biological weapons (bw) programs is a cause for alarm, particularly when they are found in developing countries in which a sense of economic and/or military inequities combines with political unrest to produce governments of unpredictable stability. The recent disclosure by Russian president Boris Yeltsin that the sudden onset of multiple cases of anthrax in Sverdlovsk in April 1979 was caused by an accidental release of organisms from a military compound in which a bw program was being pursued clearly confirmed the conclusions of many Western countries that the Soviet Union had not dismantled its bw program and was indeed in direct violation of the 1972 Biological and Toxin Weapons Convention (BWC), for which the Soviet Union was not only a signatory but actually a depositary state.[1] Later press coverage suggested the continued existence of a bw program in Russia or one of the other republics of the former Soviet Union.[2] Thus the threat from republics of the former Soviet Union remains. In addition, if the programs in the former Soviet Union are reduced or dismantled, a large number of scientists and technicians with expertise in bw development will be looking for work and could make themselves available to any country choosing to employ them. These observations, plus heightened concerns over the potential use of biological weapons during the recent Persian Gulf War, have caused a reassessment of the U.S. defensive posture to assure that its needs are met.

Current Priorities

Following renunciation of the U.S. offensive program by President Richard Nixon in 1969 and the signing of the BWC, the Biological Defense Research Program survived at a low level, sufficient only to preserve the technology base with which to conduct a more substantial defensive program at a later time if necessary. Throughout much of the 1970s the gathering and assessment of intelligence information on biological programs was conducted in a rather passive manner. In the early 1980s, however, concern over proliferation of bw programs and noncompliance with the BWC resulted in another look at intelligence information and the U.S. defensive posture. The result was an enhancement of defensive programs. But the list of potential threat agents in the early to mid-1980s was still long and diffuse. It was not until 1989 that intelligence information, gathered and assessed over several years, permitted a more focused and definitive list of threat agents.

The list that was finally developed contained many of the agents in the early U.S. program. This is to be expected because a country interested in pursuing a bw program would select those agents for which feasibility has been demonstrated. One should not, however, be surprised if additional agents are recognized. Since the U.S. offensive program was disestablished in 1969, new agents have emerged—both new in identity and new with respect to concept of production and utility. In general the U.S. offensive program, which lasted approximately 25 years, was characterized by peaks and valleys in terms of support and direction. The program was dynamic in that there was a continuous attempt to improve developed agents and pursue the development of new agents.

The technology for production of large quantities of viral agents in cell culture systems became available in the latter part of the offensive program. If the program had continued one would have expected to see viral agents that were in the research and development (R&D) phase in 1969, when the program was disestablished, become more fully developed and classified according to type in the 1970s.

Such intelligence analysis is critical—without sound and complete intelligence data, the RDT&E process would be a poorly focused use of time and money. Looking to the future, the United States must support and enhance its gathering and assessment of intelligence. In addition to the identification of facilities, people, and agents, information is essential on delivery systems, warheads, submunitions, and doctrine governing use. Of course, such information can be very difficult to acquire.

Medical protection forms a frontline defense against many biological threats. The military advantages afforded by medical protection in the form of efficacious vaccines, drugs, and diagnostic capabilities are obvious for units entering the battlefield. It is always better to prevent than have to treat, because treatment is a large consumer of resources such as medical personnel, drugs, hospital and other treatment facilities, and transportation, especially if long evacuation lines are necessary. Furthermore, if disease is prevented or even ameliorated, military units will be able to continue to fight or fight longer to accomplish their mission.

It must be noted that medical products for these purposes require an approval process established by the U.S. Food and Drug Administration just as rigorous as the pharmaceutical norm. Many vaccines have reached the "investigational" status, meaning that their efficacy and safety have been demonstrated but they can be administered only with informed consent. To overcome this obstacle to effective use in wartime, can a limited license be granted? What should the immunization policy be? Should vaccines be acquired and stockpiled? If so, which ones and how much?

Biological detectors and alarms have received high priority and should continue to do so. U.S. collaboration with some of its allies has been intense in this effort.

Laboratories should be identified and maintained to provide definitive identification of samples or specimens regardless of the source. This will assist in avoiding the confusion that arose over samples collected in the 1980s in Southeast Asia because government laboratories were not readily available to analyze subject specimens. Backup laboratories for confirmation should also be identified. The latter could be government laboratories or university laboratories that offer the specific capabilities.

Another priority is in the planning of military operations. Decision makers during Operation Desert Storm had little information or data on which to make sound decisions when faced with the task of having to destroy or neutralize Iraq's potential biological threats while at the same time minimizing the effect on coalition troops, noncombatants, and the environment. Potential targets might have included research and production facilities, missile-launched incoming warheads, low-flying aircraft with bulk tanks and dissemination capabilities, or agents stored on the ground (or underground in bunkers) in bulk, in submunitions, or in warheads. Future conflicts can be expected to produce the same problems unless appropriate information is acquired. Until the Persian Gulf War the U.S. Department of Defense gave little consideration to the means and factors involved in destruction of an enemy's biological weapons or production facilities. Simulants and mock-up bulk storage containers, submunitions, and warheads should be used to examine the effects of various munitions intended to neutralize the military utility of the agents and/or filled submunitions and warheads with minimal escape of the agent in a form that would pose a threat to the environment or noncombatants in the area. Data can be collected to assay the destructive forces that affect the neutralization of the mock-up target, including the biological agent.

Defenses and the BWC

Defensive research is a legitimate, legal activity under the BWC, and a necessary one for any state, such as the United States, that believes it and its armed forces may be subjected to bw attack. Such research is useful in reducing casualties and preventing technological surprise and thus contributes very significantly to deterring such attack in the first place. But such research may also be contentious, in part because the line between offense and defense can be obscured in military biological research, and in part because of the dual-use problem and the fact that so much legitimate bioscientific work already goes on in the commercial sector and cannot easily be monitored. The implications of these factors for the arms control regime are crucial but little understood.

Everyone is interested in assuring a dependable, worldwide ban on biological weapons—especially those who understand intimately the potential consequences of the wartime use of biological agents. During recent years organizations such as the Federation of American Scientists and, indeed, some governments have campaigned vigorously in support of a regime for verification of compliance with the BWC. The cause is noble. The adoption of a verification regime should be done, however, with great care.

It is widely recognized that verification would be extremely burdensome and intrusive. The multiplicity of laboratories devoted to work in the biological (or life) sciences is stupendous. If marginal or nominal verification schemes were adopted, the situation could be made worse, in that verification could be easily evaded. The challenge to evade the scheme may provoke the pursuit of a bw program, especially for a nation without credible deterrence capabilities in nuclear, chemical, or conventional weapons. Such a country might take the attitude, "If I can get away with it or if a loophole can be found, it is ok."

In discussing verification it has been stated, "For biological verification, the necessary focus on research rather than production requires the monitoring of *all* activities involving biological agents and the possession of *any* amount of such agents."[3] With the inclusion of pathogens and toxins harmful to animals and plants the list of agents becomes unmanageably long.

Domestic legislation enacted by the United States and some other countries makes the terms of the BWC binding on all individuals and private institutions under their jurisdiction. The laws carry heavy penalties for violations. The Third Review Conference urged all states parties to pass such legislation. A country initiating a national bw research program would do so therefore only in the most covert fashion and would have to be willing to risk worldwide condemnation regardless of its signatory status. A university undertaking even a small bw R&D project would do so with the knowledge that the law was being broken, and that the careers of the entire faculty and staff, all funding and support for the university, and the very survival of the university were being placed at great risk.

In the United States and in many other countries where the bulk of life science research is done in university laboratories, declarations under a bw verification regime would be required of a large number of universities and colleges. The inspections of university research laboratories would require a large staff, would be extremely costly, and would yield little if anything at all.

In most instances declarations and inspections would be unwelcome exercises on the university campus. Faculty are aware that they are not involved in any bw research program, that no one on the campus is involved in such a program, and that the university is unwilling to permit any research that may even have the appearance of such a program. Declarations and inspections would be annoying and time-consuming. The faculty member whose facilities and program were being declared and inspected would feel that some type of onerous label had been placed on him or her and would feel intimidated, not only by the inspectors, but also by his or her colleagues.

What happens if an inspection team finds something that was not included in the declarations? Or a quantity in excess of the limit? Or a project that leads the inspection team to become suspicious? The latter may result in investigations by the university, the funding agency, and federal and state governments. It may also trigger an investigation of the funding agency and the university. What happens to the researcher? Does he or she lose the grant? Will the federal government feel obligated to launch an investigation to determine if the law has been broken? Who pays the legal fees? Will the researcher and the university lose credibility even if the work is eventually proven to be legitimate for peaceful purposes? Will support by all agencies (federal, state, and private) for research be placed in jeopardy? Competition for research dollars is extremely tight. A good reputation that is slightly bruised by an investigation may place the institution in a less competitive posture.

Some universities contract with private companies to conduct studies on new drugs, vaccines, and diagnostic tests. Much of the information is proprietary in nature. If companies became aware that the work was being subjected to scrutiny and inspection by a team of international inspectors, they might abandon the contractual arrangements with universities. The work would not escape inspection within the company, but the company might feel it had better control.

One can predict that some faculty simply will not tolerate inspections. They would stop the research before submitting to inspection for purposes of verifying compliance with the BWC. If a faculty member refuses to cooperate, should he or she be considered guilty, like the driver who refuses to take the breath alcohol test? Is the university guilty? If legitimate research is stopped because a researcher refuses to tolerate the inspection hassle or feels that his or her integrity is being challenged beyond the tolerable level, a brain drain from biomedical research may result.

Let us look at a hypothetical but realistic scenario. A comprehensive verification regime is developed and put in place. The focus is research on pathogens and toxins affecting humans, animals, and plants. All major research universities are affected. Annual declarations are made and inspections follow. Hundreds of laboratories or research programs are inspected and nothing is found except for a few instances in which the quantity of the agents exceeds the limit because a researcher had to produce a large quantity of the organism to extract a workable quantity of sugar from the wall of the organism or an outbreak of anthrax in wildlife and cattle resulted in a transfer without notification of multiple strains of the causative organism to a neighboring country collaborating in the control of the outbreak. The scientific community, alerted to the fact that a major component of the community is being hassled, the cost of the endeavor is overwhelming, and the yield is nil, launches a counterattack. Large professional organizations representing the scientific community, such as the American Society for Microbiology and the American Association for the Advancement of Science, have sufficient political clout to initiate an effort to bring a halt to costly, unproductive verification activities. How will the country respond? Could it be forced to drop from the BWC? Will legislators feel they have been duped?

Who pays the high cost of verification? Will poor, developing countries refuse to participate? Will they drop out of the treaty? Will additional nations not join? With the appearance of new nations and the newly gained independence of others, might they choose not to accede to the BWC because of the hassle and expense? Such countries might be the very countries in which activities should be watched with suspicion. Remember that biological weapons have been referred to as "the poor man's atomic bomb." If costs were passed on to the laboratory being inspected, overhead costs for research would go even higher. This could have a devastating effect on universities and the agencies supporting the research.

University faculty, who enjoy academic freedom and consider it a good that must be preserved at all costs, frequently collaborate with colleagues around the world. Professional acquaintances result in exchange of information, visits, and, in the case of biomedical sciences, an exchange of disease agents. If verification were to have a negative impact on the exchanges, academia might revolt, progress on cures for some of the most dreaded diseases might be slowed, and the goals conceived under Article X of the BWC might never be realized.

During the Second and Third Review Conferences on the BWC much was accomplished to enhance the effectiveness of the treaty. With a rapidly changing world it may be important to allow the politically binding confidence-building measures to work and benefits to be assessed before changing the treaty or adding major amendments that may cause collapse.

Conclusion

The United States will continue to be looked to as the leader in bw defense. Close collaboration with the United Kingdom and Canada, which has been traditional, will continue to enhance the effort. Other countries with small but active programs include Germany, France, and Sweden. It is possible that Russia (and possibly one or more of the other republics of the former Soviet Union) may be willing to open its program to full examination and to actively share its bw defensive program.

The utility of biological weapons may be a nonissue in considering certain aspects of biodefense. Even if it can be argued that such weapons have limited utility, any country that elects to pursue a bw program poses a threat. Also, poorly developed and poorly delivered weapons may still be a threat for which defensive measures must be developed.

Advances in biotechnology in the past decade could potentially alter the threat. Although it may be possible through genetic engineering to produce "a wolf in sheep's clothing," the threat from application of genetic engineering would first come from the production of selected protein toxins that could not be produced readily by other means. Minimal alterations of organisms to enhance such factors as virulence and stability should also be expected.

Finally, it is important to underscore that in the past biological defense for the most part has been directed appropriately toward medical protection and individual or collective physical protection. The products have been drugs, vaccines, masks, protective garments, and diagnostic and detection devices. In Desert Storm the threat became a launched SCUD missile with a nonconventional warhead. Theater missile defense took on a new dimension. The objective then was destruction with minimal impact on friendly troops, noncombatants, and the environment. Missile defense continues to be a major concern to military planners; it is, therefore, important that strong consideration be given to the biological threat. A parallel concern is the targeting of biological production and storage facilities with minimal effect on noncombatants and the environment. Future conflicts must be expected to involve a biological threat.

Notes

1. *Washington Post,* June 16, 1992.

2. Ibid., August 13, 1992.

3. Barbara Hatch Rosenberg and Gordon Burck, "Verification of Compliance with the Biological Weapons Convention," in Susan Wright, ed., *Preventing a Biological Arms Race* (Cambridge, Mass.: MIT Press, 1990), 300–329.

8
New Challenges and New Policy Priorities for the 1990s
Brad Roberts

Anyone who has toiled away on the problem of chemical weapons (cw) well remembers its relative obscurity during the cold war, with its emphasis on issues of nuclear warfare and arms control. But if cw issues have stood in the shadows over the years, issues related to biological weapons (bw) have been nearly invisible. At most, they command only sporadic attention from policymakers. In the research community, little serious thought has been done, or at least committed to paper. Furthermore, the issue has been stigmatized, and the sharp abhorrence attaching to biological weapons has tended to politicize and narrow what public dialogue has occurred.

Yet biological weapons loom large in the post–cold war security environment. The near brush with biological warfare at the hands of the Iraqis in the Persian Gulf War awakened military experts to the continued perils of biological weapons and alerted everyone to the larger problem of bw proliferation. In the United States, signs of a renewed interest in problems of biological warfare are evident in the executive branch, where both the Pentagon and the State Department have revisited key issues in the last year or two, as well as in the Congress, where the House is studying and evaluating the policy agenda. The bw issue is also of growing interest outside the United States, among a diplomatic community increasingly eager to stem the proliferation of biological weapons, as well as among security experts in the Middle East, South Asia, and East Asia uncertain of the impact of bw proliferation within their regions.

Indeed, it is not uncommon today to hear biological weapons touted as a major challenge for the post–cold war era. The proliferation of unconventional and advanced conventional military capability is indeed a central feature of the interna-

68

tional security environment of the 1990s. But it seems to this observer that biological weapons are virtually an afterthought in the litany of "nuclear, chemical, and biological," something added to the rhetoric without any sense of the content of the subject. Indeed, there is a very striking tendency to equate problems of bw proliferation, control, and deterrence with their chemical or nuclear counterparts. This is a mistake because it obscures unique characteristics of the bw problem.

This chapter offers a review of the bw issue in general policy terms in an effort to sketch out some of these characteristics. It begins with a brief overview of the basic policy approach adopted in 1969 that continues to shape U.S. policy today, one that balances military priorities with diplomatic measures, including the Biological and Toxin Weapons Convention (BWC). It then evaluates the challenges to existing bw policies as they have emerged in the intervening years. These include bw proliferation, the biotechnology revolution, terrorism, and the changing compliance debate. The chapter then turns to the future of U.S. policy and discusses ways in which policy might evolve in response to changing circumstances. Overall, the chapter constitutes the editor's attempt to distill and integrate the policy implications of the other essays in this volume. Analogies to the chemical and nuclear domains are employed where useful, but the important differences between them and the biological domain are explicitly drawn out.

The Existing Policy Framework

Biological weapons are munitions or other delivery systems, such as spray tanks, filled with biological agents of warfare—living organisms, whatever their nature, or infective materials derived from them—that are intended to cause disease or death among humans, animals, and/or plants and that depend for their effect on their ability to multiply in the organism attacked. Toxins are chemical substances produced by biological systems but are not themselves living.[1]

Biological weapons are not new to public policy. A century ago diplomats were concerned that poisonous gases and analogous materials, including bacteriological methods of warfare, might be used on the battlefield. They sought to ban such weapons as part of the general international effort of that era to codify the rules of war and eliminate unnecessary suffering. Their efforts resulted in the Brussels Declaration of 1874 and the Hague Conferences of 1899 and 1907. Although chemical weapons were used extensively in World War I by each of the major combatants, biological weapons were not used. Public abhorrence of the use of chemical weapons and general concern about armaments and arms races as sources of international instability led to creation of the Geneva Protocol of 1925, more formally known as the Protocol for the Prohibition of the Use in War of Asphyxiating, Poisonous or Other Gases, and of Bacteriological Methods of Warfare. Note that this is a ban on use, not possession.[2]

The threat of biological warfare became more concrete during World War II, when the intelligence agencies of the Allies detected bw preparations by the Axis powers. This stimulated first an investigation of the feasibility of the battlefield use of biological weapons, and second, once this was confirmed by both U.S. and British investigators in field tests with anthrax, steps to create a stockpile of biological weapons for possible use in retaliation should Germany or Japan use them first. The only reported use of biological weapons during World War II was on an experimental basis by elements of the Japanese Imperial Army operating in Manchuria.[3] Thus U.S. and British bw stockpiles were built but not used, and they were destroyed in the years after the war.

But research and development (R&D) programs for both offensive and defensive bw purposes continued in the United States and Britain, as elsewhere, and received increased priority with the buildup of the Soviet military threat in the 1950s and concern about a Soviet bw arsenal. But the programs of the two countries moved in divergent directions.[4] Facing sharp resource constraints, Britain opted to abandon both chemical and biological weapons (cbw) in favor of reliance on nuclear retaliation and protective gear. The United States resumed production of biological weapons (while continuing cw production) and developed a doctrine for their use.

In 1969, the United States abandoned this approach. The Nixon administration unilaterally renounced the possession of

biological weapons and undertook to destroy the existing
stockpile while seeking a similar commitment from the Soviet
Union. This decision was based on four factors.[5] One was the
political impulse to build a new relationship with the USSR;
joint biological disarmament was valued in the White House as
an early, relatively low-risk step on the path to détente.

A second factor was related to the utility of biological
weapons. Their unpredictability on the battlefield made them
unlikely tactical instruments for U.S. military commanders,
even if used in retaliation. For strategic applications—meaning
massive attack against cities or economic infrastructure—the
unpredictability of biological agents was less important. But
biological weapons were essentially redundant to a state
possessing nuclear weapons; an ability to retaliate in kind
seemed unnecessary as a response to a Soviet bw attack on a
nuclear-armed United States. The nuclear retaliatory threat
could therefore be seen as a credible deterrent to bw attack.
In retrospect, some analysts infer from this decision that the
United States abandoned biological weapons because they are
useless. This is a misreading of a decision that the specific
military effects of biological agents were marginal, if not
irrelevant, to a United States equipped with other conventional
and nuclear assets and not confronting an imminent military
threat.

A third factor related to safety. Biological weapons were
dangerous to stockpile, carrying the risk that their accidental
release might kill large numbers of people. No immediate
military threat seemed to justify running such a risk.

A fourth factor related to the possible spread of such
weapons. It was believed that the United States would be
better served by nipping in the bud any possible interest in
biological weapons elsewhere in the world than by maintaining
an active offensive program that might stimulate such interest.

The implications of the policy initiatives of 1969 include
the following. First, in-kind deterrence was abandoned in favor
of the possibility of nuclear retaliation. Note, however, that in-
kind deterrence was deemed necessary at the chemical level,
given the view that chemical weapons were more credible
battlefield instruments than biological weapons and that a

state enjoying the one-sided use of chemical weapons in a conflict could easily control the pace and character of the battle—
thus increasing its incentives to use them. Second, increased
emphasis was given to defensive measures in the form of
personal protection gear and vaccines for field use. Such
defenses were seen as necessary to hedge against the surprise
use of biological weapons in attacks on U.S. forces or population centers, while the concomitant research was seen as a
valuable deterrent of the ambitions of those who might think
that a few biological weapons could go a long way against U.S.
forces. For this reason, some degree of transparency in the bw
research program has been emphasized from that time on.

Third, the United States and its allies became willing to
settle for an arms control measure that had only the barest of
verification and compliance provisions. Because they were
confident that the Soviets shared U.S. perceptions of the
limited utility of biological weapons and of the supremacy of
nuclear weapons in strategic doctrine, and encouraged by the
prevailing détente, they were not much concerned about a
strategic surprise by a noncompliant USSR and hence placed
little emphasis on rigorous arms control in this area. The
result was a bilateral agreement that became the basis for the
multilateral BWC, known formally as the Convention on the
Prohibition of the Development, Production and Stockpiling of
Bacteriological (Biological) and Toxin Weapons and on Their
Destruction. Signed on April 10, 1972, it entered into force
three years later, on March 26, 1975, with the United States
sharing duties as a repository state with the USSR and Britain.
Under the terms of the convention, the parties undertake not
to develop, produce, stockpile, or acquire biological agents or
toxins "of types and in quantities that have no justification for
prophylactic, protective, and other peaceful purposes," as well
as weapons and means of delivery. By 1990, there were 112
signatories, although a few states (Iraq among them) had failed
to deposit instruments of ratification.

This basic policy framework combining specific forms of
military readiness with specific types of arms control remains
in place today. Among the general community of policymakers
and scholars concerned with problems of international secu-

rity, it is also fair to say that this is where thinking about the bw problem stopped. Not many have explored how the approach adopted in 1969 might have been affected by the changing times and by the end of the cold war and the Persian Gulf conflict of 1991 in particular.

Sporadically during the intervening years, however, a few experts have taken an interest in the issue. Pursuit of arms control required the U.S. diplomatic community to engage in BWC review conferences in 1979, 1986, and 1991. More generally, concern about the effectiveness of the treaty has grown, especially about how to address doubts about compliance. A noteworthy accretion of related policy actions has also occurred, such as the Australia Group's work, beginning in 1989, to limit trade in the materials and technology necessary for bw production.

The military track has also commanded occasional attention.[6] In 1980 the Defense Science Board criticized the bw defensive research program as poorly focused and underfunded. In 1985 the U.S. Chemical Warfare Review Commission, stepping beyond its mandate in order to voice concerns about biological weapons, argued that "the Department of Defense does not have an adequate grasp of the biological-warfare threat and has not been giving it sufficient attention. Both intelligence and research in this area, though improved after a virtual halt during the 1970s, are strikingly deficient."[7] In 1991, only days before the beginning of the action to expel Iraq from Kuwait, the U.S. General Accounting Office issued a report, suppressed at the time, that detailed potentially crippling deficiencies in the battlefield preparedness of U.S. forces in face of potential Iraqi use of chemical and biological weapons.[8]

The strategic, military, technical, and political context of bw deterrence and control has changed markedly in the last two and a half decades. If U.S. policy—and the international efforts of which it is an integral part—is to remain effective in the years ahead, complacency about existing approaches must be set aside. Before policy can be sharply focused, the implications of the new factors must be understood. The following sections discuss four of these factors in turn.

Proliferation

Despite the hope that biological disarmament by the super-
powers and creation of the BWC would halt any possible
interest in biological weapons, bw proliferation has evidently
proceeded. Ten or 11 countries have been detected by Western intelligence agencies as engaged in offensive bw programs,[9]
up from just 4 in the 1960s (of which 2 were the United States
and the USSR). (This compares with roughly 20 states of
concern in connection with the proliferation of chemical
weapons and 8 to 10 in the nuclear area.) Those publicly
identified by U.S. government sources include Iraq, Iran, Syria,
Libya, the People's Republic of China, North Korea, and Tai-
wan.[10] Officials have also made a general statement that of
those suspected of pursuing bw programs, some are in the
Middle East, some are known sponsors of terrorism, and some
are signatories of the BWC.[11]

Fears of bw proliferation also stem from the collapse of the
USSR and the fear, parallel to that in the nuclear domain, that
the biological weapons of the former Soviet military will trickle
out to other states (or non-state entities) or that the expertise
to produce biological weapons will be purchased from unem-
ployed and hungry Soviet scientists. Reports of efforts to
acquire such expertise and weapons have floated in the Russian press.[12]

The factors stimulating such proliferation probably closely
parallel those in the chemical area. Declining barriers to
acquisition have played a role, particularly with the steady
diffusion of dual-use technologies. Regional conflict and strategic need have also provided incentives because regional leaders have sought the means to deter well-armed neighbors or
outside interveners, to coerce regional adversaries, or to seek
victory in war. The difficulty of acquiring nuclear capabilities
and the increasing political costs of chemical weapons, as well
as their not inconsequential fiscal costs, may have stimulated
specific interest in biological weapons in countries that pose a
general proliferation risk. Mere curiosity may also explain
some of the research work, as some developing countries seek

to understand the possible military applications of the new biological sciences increasingly within their reach.

The discovery of Iraq's bw program, which Iraqi officials have acknowledged was intended for purposes of offense and not defense, helped awaken the international community to these trends in proliferation.[13] But the continuing debate within the United Nations Special Commission on Iraq (UNSCOM) about the character and scale of Iraq's bw program echoes a similar debate in the chemical area; that is, what are the implications of simple statements about numbers of proliferators? Are all proliferators of equal significance?

In the chemical domain, of the 20 or so countries rumored to have offensive cw programs, perhaps only as few as one-third actually possess militarily significant operational capabilities.[14] In the biological domain, countries evidently have been termed bw proliferators when quantities of infective materials have been discovered for which no peaceful purposes are discernible. Various thresholds can be identified as determining military significance. They range from R&D to the proofing of weapon concepts, test production, scaling up of production capability, stockpiling of agent, weaponization, stockpiling of weapons, preparation of delivery systems, creation of the doctrine for use, and training. One further factor is that a significant bw program would probably also entail the acquisition of and training with protective measures; not every developing state will share the military and public safety concerns of the developed countries, but many will find some protective measures prudent if only to preserve secrecy by preventing detectable health problems. In the R&D phase itself, there are important differences between programs that emphasize the simple agents found in the stockpiles of some industrialized countries in the 1940s and 1950s, the more sophisticated agents that were the focus of U.S. interest in the late 1960s, and the novelties made possible by bioengineering. Of course, even a stockpile or capability deemed to be fairly rudimentary can be militarily significant in certain circumstances and thus is not to be lightly dismissed. Further analysis of these factors in terms of the bw proliferation problem would help to bring the problem into sharper focus but cannot be performed so long as the necessary data remain classified.

The primary effect of bw proliferation at this point is to give a new level of urgency to the general bw issue. It also raises a number of questions about current policy. First, it casts doubt on the effectiveness of the BWC as an instrument of international security. Second, it raises questions about U.S. military planning priorities and about whether an approach crafted in an era dominated by the superpower conflict and the remote risk of biological warfare remains the best guarantee of the security and safety of the United States and its military forces. These questions are equally valid for other states that, under the aegis of collective security or unilaterally, may seek to project power into regions where biological warfare may be inflicted upon them. The risk of such attack may be seen to raise the costs of intervention, but the possibility that such threats may be used coercively within a region or projected beyond it may heighten the incentive to intervene.

The Biotechnology Revolution

The second key change since the 1960s in the strategic context of bw policy is the revolution that has occurred in the biological sciences. Advances in genetic manipulation and the availability of more sophisticated technologies for working with biological materials have had a profound and positive impact on health care and agricultural development but they have military implications that are as yet not widely understood.

The biotechnology revolution has made it possible to create novel biological organisms, potentially far more lethal than any of the traditional bw agents. Conceivably that technology might also make it possible at some future time to craft agents that harm only specific racial groups. But such ideas appear far-fetched as yet and novel agents probably do not represent the most salient short-term problem because the difficulties of developing them are substantial.[15] Rather, the key factor is that advances in biotechnology have made it easier to do a number of things that in the 1960s seemed difficult or risky. For example, militarily significant quantities of biological agent can be produced much more quickly, obviating the need to stockpile large amounts for extended periods. This makes it more risky to misjudge the intent behind bw R&D programs, increases their potential strategic salience, and decreases the likelihood that intelligence or arms control inspections will detect significant capabilities. This weakens confidence that bw programs in the developing world hold no surprises of potentially strategic consequences. Better agents, meaning ones that act more quickly or are less suscep- tible to degradation by exposure to the environment, matched to more effective delivery systems—especially cruise missiles —may make the tactical use of biological agents less unpre- dictable and more likely, especially if the attacking country also has sufficiently robust biological defenses to inoculate its forces to protect them from the effect of the weapons it uses.[16]

The dual-use character of biological technology and facili- ties also makes it increasingly difficult to distinguish between military and commercial facilities. Moreover, the increasing availability of biotechnology and advanced expertise means that perhaps as many as 100 countries have the means of making their own biological weapons without depending on exports from the advanced industrial countries.[17]

Thus, the primary effect of the biotechnology revolution has been to raise questions about some of the assumptions and perceptions that underpin U.S. policy—especially the view that anyone studying biological weapons is likely to conclude, as the United States did, that their utility is narrow and diffi- cult to achieve. The revolution and its implications also cast doubt on the ability of the international community even to keep track of the proliferation problem.

Terrorism

BW proliferation and the biotechnology revolution have also aggravated a problem of long standing—the threat that terror- ists will use biological weapons. Happily, biological agents have not been the weapon of choice for terrorists so far, and there are no recorded instances of successful bw attack by terrorists. This may have to do with technical factors. For example, contamination of a municipal water supply would require compensation for a significant dilution factor and hence quantities of biological agent beyond what terrorists might find it easy to acquire or transport (in any case such supplies are already carefully screened for contamination). It may have also to do with the political context of terrorism. Terrorists apparently prefer bloody weapons that make good public theater and therefore draw attention to their claims through the media rather than weapons generally deemed abhorrent that might delegitimize their cause.[18]

Even so, the prospects for bw terrorism have probably increased as sponsors of terrorism have acquired bw agents and weapons and as dual-use technology and expertise have spread internationally. The prospects have also probably increased with the end of the cold war. The collapse of state structures in the former Communist world and the rise of ethnic conflict have increased the number of non-state actors seeking to annihilate hated enemies, keep out intervening forces, and manipulate international will. Biological weapons might be seen as useful for each of these tasks. The risks of attacks on the United States specifically may have increased as well. As the "last superpower" and primary defender of the international status quo, the United States is a likely target, made more likely by its reputation among some as a skittish or fickle power whose political decisions are determined fundamentally by media that magnify the effects of acts of violence. The scenarios whereby such attacks might be perpetrated on the United States, or its allies, are truly chilling, and even if the past is a source of consolation, the present raises some very disturbing possibilities.[19]

Compliance Problems

A final factor in the changing strategic context are deepening doubts about the effectiveness of the existing treaty regime in detecting and responding to non-compliant actions by states parties. This problem has been brought into sharp focus during the last two years by two problem countries: Iraq and Russia.

Iraq's ability to pursue a bw program without international detection illustrates the ease with which surreptitious programs can be conducted, as well as the indifference of most countries, even in the presence of strong evidence that something was amiss and of Iraq's known uses of chemical weapons.[20] Continuing uncertainties about Iraq's bw program underscore the dubious ability of even highly intrusive inspections to uncover patterns of activity and resolve doubts about compliance.

Russia inherited the bw programs of the USSR, and the old problem of Soviet compliance lingers there today. Soviet compliance with its bilateral commitment to the United States to abandon biological weapons was taken virtually taken for granted in the early détente period, but doubts soon emerged. The outbreak of anthrax in Sverdlovsk in 1979 galvanized the concern of U.S. policymakers and interested allies. Reports of the use of biological agents and toxins by Soviet proxies in Southeast Asia in the late 1970s and by Soviet forces in Afghanistan in the 1980s—the so-called yellow rain allegations—only heightened these concerns.[21] U.S. governmental charges were challenged by private researchers,[22] and a healthy debate continued in the context of the larger, highly politicized U.S. debate about the "evil empire."

Boris Yeltsin has acknowledged that the Soviet Union "lagged" in implementing its commitment under the BWC to destroy existing biological weapons and conduct research only for defensive purposes. During his visit to Camp David in February 1992, he said that past military efforts had "crossed the line" set out by international treaties.[23] Yeltsin himself had been Communist Party boss in Sverdlovsk at the time of the anthrax outbreak and has alleged that he was misled about the nature of the accident and purposes of the facility until some time later.[24]

Yeltsin's acknowledgment of violations means that the Soviet military had crossed beyond legitimate R&D of protective and prophylactic measures into production of biological agents and delivery systems. This was subsequently confirmed by Anatoly Kuntsevich, chairman of a Russian presidential committee on chemical and biological weapons, who reported that "after ratification of the convention, offensive programs in the sphere of biological weapons were not immediately stopped, the research and production continued. . . . Researchers continued to develop combat biological agents and means of their delivery by aircraft and missiles."[25] Evidently, only in 1985 under Mikhail Gorbachev did the Defense Ministry begin to bring its bw activities into alignment with BWC commitments although the violations evidently extended through the

Gorbachev years and have only ceased—if in fact they have—
with Boris Yeltsin's commitment to cease funding such
programs.[26]

Informed Russian sources say that no significant stockpiles
of biological agents or weapons were accumulated, although a
limited number of production facilities were constructed—
assertions echoed in Russia's report on past offensive and
defensive programs made in conjunction with the confidence-
building measure (CBM) adopted at the BWC Review Conference of September 1991. It has also been reported that more
than a score of facilities devoted to research, production,
storage, and testing of biological agents have been identified by
U.S. intelligence agencies.[27] Gruesome reports have also
emerged that in the 1940s and 1950s the NKVD conducted bw
experiments on unwitting prisoners in the Gulag—leading to
their deaths. Finally, the number of personnel in military
biological programs has reportedly been cut by 50 percent and
funding for relevant research cut by 30 percent, and the
Russian Defense Ministry's department for offensive bw work
has been dismantled.[28]

Doubts linger in the West about Russia's claims that no
weapons were ever produced and that all activities have been
brought to a halt. Moreover, Westerners worry that the political leadership in Moscow may be unable to get from the military either full disclosure or a firm commitment to cease all bw
activities beyond those permitted by the BWC.

The United States, Russia, and Britain agreed in September
1992 on an ad hoc measure to help resolve some of these
doubts and problems. It commits Russia to opening suspect
facilities to inspection, converting bw facilities to civilian
production, and ending bw projects except for defensive
programs. It provides for mutual inspections of biological sites
in the three countries. U.S. and British officials will visit any
suspect site and conduct inspections as intrusive as necessary
to resolve concerns. Russian inspectors will be permitted to
visit U.S. and British civilian biological research facilities once
the initial round of inspections inside Russia is completed.

This unhappy tale is important not just for what it tells us
about the cold war or Russia's current tribulations. It also

raises fundamental questions about the BWC. Although it provides for recourse to the United Nations (UN) Security Council in the event that cooperation among states parties does not resolve compliance concerns, the treaty has been left without an effective compliance mechanism, and the regime has been paralyzed in dealing with such concerns. The ability of both the USSR and Iraq to hide a large program from the international community for years and in the case of the USSR from its own political leadership for a shorter period also raises questions about the efficacy of the convention vis-à-vis totalitarian or dysfunctional states. The continuing political and intelligence challenge of sorting out the exact contours of the Soviet/Russian bw program—and exactly what happened at Sverdlovsk, which is still unresolved[29]—underscores the lesson learned by UNSCOM in Iraq: verification is a complex political and technological process that involves much more than monitoring and requires the kinds of investigation of patterns of activity possible only over extended periods of time. This story is also a damning indictment of an international community that could not muster the political will to deal effectively with allegations of Soviet and Iraqi noncompliance, either by resolving those charges to their mutual satisfaction or undertaking to secure compliance once cheating was proven. It is the failure of the politics of compliance that could have the longest-term consequences, and that failure is what is being tested by Iraq today.

In light of this review, what policies should the United States pursue and with what sorts of priorities for the coming years?

The Future Direction of Military Policy

There is little in the foregoing analysis to suggest that the basic policies of the United States dealing with the military aspects of the bw problem should be changed. A mix of measures to defend and deter remains relevant, but some priorities should be adjusted.

Some commentators have cited the proliferation of biological weapons as a reason to halt research on bw defenses in the United States and indeed to amend the BWC to prevent such work. Arguing that the fine line between defense and offense is nearly impossible to define and enforce in military R&D programs and that an active R&D program encourages interest in offensive bw capabilities, they prescribe abandonment of all research.[30] This is a distinctly minority view and undervalues the utility of protective measures on the battlefield and as a deterrent while overstating the salience of U.S. activities as a stimulus to proliferation. It is doubtful that such a step would have any result other than denuding the United States of effective defenses while piquing interest among potential U.S. adversaries in capitalizing on that vulnerability.

But the defensive R&D program has not been as successful as it should have been in preparing U.S. forces for combat on a contaminated battlefield. The General Accounting Office, the Joint Chiefs of Staff, and the Office of the Secretary of Defense have each recently criticized the low level of protection afforded U.S. troops.[31] Noteworthy, for example, is the fact that detectors for even the most common biological agents are not available for field deployment and that supplies of effective antidotes do not exist for even some existing bw agents. Also of note is the steadily shrinking commercial industrial base for vaccine production, largely because of the commercial risks associated with the ever growing threat of litigation. The United States needs to give priority to improvements over the full range of bw defense—detectors, protective gear, vaccines and other prophylactic measures, and the R&D support base.[32]

Even with some rectification of these deficiencies, it is important to understand that bw defenses are useful primarily as a deterrent. Protective gear cannot be improved to the point that its burdensome aspects, such as the heat fatigue and dehydration caused by rubberized gear, would be eliminated. Nor will even the most comprehensive program provide 100 percent certainty of protection. Thus even with the most sophisticated defenses, U.S. commanders would not choose to initiate biological warfare operations and would probably seek to avoid a biologically contaminated battlefield whenever possible. Defenses are important because they raise the threshold at which cheating by an opponent becomes militarily relevant, exactly as they do in the chemical area. They do this by narrowing the range of bw agents of possible military utility and by requiring a potential aggressor to field large quantities of effective agent in reliable delivery systems. Because such activities are moot against targets that have been inoculated, an R&D program also deters states from thinking that they might easily field a bw agent that the United States could not quickly recognize and treat. This point helps also to explain both the value of transparency in the research program, which is to signal and deter, and its limits, because uncertainty about the vaccines quickly available to U.S. forces must be preserved and access to U.S. programs must be denied to those who would exploit them for spinoffs with possible offensive applications.

Research on infectious diseases remains a military priority whatever the degree of likelihood of confronting biological agents of warfare on the battlefield. The military, like humanity as a whole, faces many biological hazards. Globally, over 2 billion people are currently infected with vaccine-preventable diseases; 3 billion carry other infectious and parasitic diseases; more than 40 million people die each year from disease.[33] Both the vaccines provided U.S. forces entering Somalia in autumn 1992 and the importance of their ready availability are reminders of this problem and of the variety of national and international institutions whose interests bear on the larger subject of biological research and the military.

The bw terrorism challenge also raises the question of whether bw defenses have been too narrowly confined to specifically battlefield concerns and whether it might not be prudent to expand protection to the civilian population more generally. In the 1950s and 1960s the United States implemented a broad-reaching civil defense program to limit the consequences of a possible Soviet nuclear attack. A program of this scale is not warranted by the current biological threat and in any case would not be politically sustainable in an era defined by the post–cold war peace, absent a cataclysmic event to reshape perceptions. But given the proliferation and terrorism factors discussed above, the United States would be well advised to rethink its degree of preparation for this contingency. It would be useful to investigate whether the Centers for Disease Control would be capable of responding to the simultaneous outbreak of disease in multiple cities, or what would be required to give it such a backup capability. Some type of emergency preparedness to respond to and investigate bw terrorist threats akin to those created long ago in the nuclear domain and more recently in the chemical area would be prudent.[34]

Given the fundamental changes in the geostrategic environment since the 1960s and in the technological and political assumptions underpinning the policy initiatives of 1969, it is logical to question whether the United States should restore an in-kind retaliatory capability.[35] After all, the decision to forgo biological weapons was crafted with a specific cold war–vintage threat clearly in mind and détente made a certain risk taking seem worthwhile, with the nuclear arsenal seemed a ready backup. The end of the cold war has probably made it more likely that biological weapons will be used in regional wars and against the United States or its forces. Moreover, the credibility of the threat to use nuclear weapons for reasons other than national survival has diminished substantially since the heyday of the cold war, and a U.S. president might face overwhelming political disincentives to using them in the developing world even where a strong military rationale exists. On the other hand, the United States has a strong commitment to respond vigorously to any use of such weapons.

It is doubtful, however, that a bw retaliatory capability would add much to the deterrence of bw attack where such an attack is a tangible problem for the United States. For a strategic attack on the United States with unconventional weapons of any kind, the nuclear force remains a credible retaliatory instrument. The key question is whether and in what way bw proliferation in the developing world actually matters to U.S. military operations and force planning choices. Improved protective gear and a stronger research program still offer a great deal of bw deterrence, as do conventional forces and improvements to theater air defenses. When and if deterrence collapses, and U.S. forces are attacked with biological weapons, the superior mobility and conventional preponderance of U.S. forces—if they can be brought to bear in timely fashion— should significantly ameliorate any possible short-term negative tactical consequences, just as in the chemical area.[36] A bw retaliatory capability would add little to this list of assets and would probably never be implemented by local commanders, who would prefer instead to shorten the time their troops must spend with biological weapons on the battlefield. And if the United States were to resume the capacity for bw retaliation it would do so at substantial cost—abrogation of the BWC, open and more extensive bw proliferation, and thus a sharp increase in the bw threat to U.S. forces.

In sum, the argument for recreating a bw retaliatory capability is weak, resting only on a changing strategic environment and the notional benefits of in-kind deterrence. A much stronger argument exists for relying on other means of deterrence backed by strong protective measures.

Two additional initiatives in support of this military agenda would be useful. One would emphasize intelligence. U.S. military (and diplomatic) strategies would be well served by a better definition of the bw threat. The CIA has taken steps to improve its capacities in this regard with the creation of the Center for Nonproliferation in January 1992. But the traditional threat assessments are reputed to probe little beyond surface factors. Nothing in the public domain suggests that the United States or its allies have developed a sufficient capability to identify patterns in the biological activities in suspect countries, to evaluate changes in those patterns, or to assess standards of containment or competence to conduct genetic manipulations.

The other initiative would be in the area of preemption. In time of war or near war, the United States needs to be able to destroy bw production and storage facilities without also risking widespread contamination. It managed this well in the Persian Gulf War of 1991, but only with a good deal of improvisation. But in instances short of open war, where states are arming terrorists for attack with biological weapons or are themselves attempting covert strikes, the United States should also have the means to disrupt and destroy bw facilities without recourse to the open use of military power.

A final concern relates to the organization of the U.S. government to implement this strategy. Authority within the military community on bw issues is remarkably diffuse. In the 1970s a similar problem was recognized in the chemical area, with the result that a deputy assistant secretary's position was created in the Office of the Secretary of Defense to coordinate cw policy. That office has been charged with the bw issue as well, which is natural given the many parallels in the issues of military preparedness for both forms of warfare, but bw concerns have necessarily taken a back seat to the much higher profile cw issue over the last decade. The army has responsibility as lead agency for each of the armed services on cbw issues, but it too has tended to give priority to cw matters. The bulk of the bw R&D budget is dispersed to nongovernmental research entities that together do not comprise a single bureaucratic entity. Some administrative means should be found to improve the management and oversight of the military's bw programs and to ensure stable funding and consistent political support. This is separate from the strategic task of reexamining at the national level each aspect of a comprehensive policy approach to dealing with new challenges.

The Future of BW Arms Control

The new challenges of the 1970s, 1980s, and 1990s have only increased the importance of arms control to management of the bw problem. The Biological Weapons Convention's importance as a norm of international politics has also increased with the breakdown of the stable cold war international security structure and the rise of ethnic violence by non-state actors.

The limitations of the BWC have been well recognized and on three occasions states parties to the treaty have met together in review conferences to consider the performance of the convention and possible measures to strengthen it. In 1979, discussion focused on doubts about Soviet compliance, with the United States releasing information about the outbreak of anthrax at Sverdlovsk.[37] In 1986 the focus was on CBMs, given the then-prevalent view that the primary problem dogging the convention was not noncompliance but the failure of most states to take any interest in the regime and thus to raise doubts about its value.[38] CBMs were adopted calling for a variety of declarations and undertakings, the general purpose of which was to bring the international regime to the level of openness and transparency exercised by the United States. In 1991, there was no single focus. Instead, braced by the near brush with biological warfare in the Persian Gulf War, the worsening news of proliferation, and Yeltsin's confessions, delegates met to discuss a broad set of issues.[39] New CBMs were added, including a "null declaration," so that states with no bw facilities or programs would still have an obligation to demonstrate compliance and thus participate in the regime; prior to the Third Review Conference, only 17 developing countries had complied with the CBMs adopted at the second. The United States, among others, also made a strong diplomatic effort to reaffirm the BWC as a moral norm.

The sharpest area of disagreement at the third conference was on the wish of many states to add verification provisions to the BWC.[40] On this subject the United States found itself in notable isolation from its traditional allies. The political impetus to add such provisions had many sources. Between the second and third conferences, perceptions of the basic challenge confronting the BWC seem to have shifted markedly— the problem was no longer seen as a failure of confidence but had become a failure of compliance. Iraq's bw program raised questions about how many of the proliferating states might actually be building bw arsenals for military purposes, which increased an interest in both detecting and deterring such endeavors. Views seemed to be coalescing that a right to intrusive inspections could fill this need, given the shift by the governing board of the International Atomic Energy Agency (IAEA) toward more intrusive inspections of nuclear facilities and UNSCOM's experience investigating Iraq's bw program. Many of the participants in the Third Review Conference were also participating in the chemical disarmament negotiations in Geneva, which in summer 1991 were working out a compromise verification system for the Chemical Weapons Convention (CWC) under negotiation there. This led many to hope that the CWC verification regime could be easily reformulated and tacked on to the BWC. Thus the United States found itself swimming against the tide of opinion.

It was no accident that verification provisions were not included in the BWC when it was drafted over two decades ago, nor was it merely willful obstructionism that compelled the United States to assert its opposition to such provisions with considerable fervor in 1991. As argued above, the challenge of detecting militarily significant activity in the biologi-cal area is arguably far more difficult than in the chemical, nuclear, or conventional areas. The technology necessary to create and manufacture biological weapons is virtually all dual-use in character, unlike nuclear technology, which requires large, dedicated facilities for weapons pro-grams, or the chemical domain, where the most worrisome chemicals have few or no civilian applications. Thus signatures for specifically bw facilities are very difficult to find. This problem is complicated by the fact that R&D is permitted—and necessary—under the BWC for defensive purposes. Thus, even if a facility is identified as producing some bw agent and inspections confirm this fact, there is no guarantee of deter-mining a violation.

The United States faces a special challenge in this regard. Because of its commitment to transparency, a great deal of the work done on vaccines in the United States is contracted out to universities, where the work is monitored but where its political context is highly volatile.[41] Moreover, a comprehen-sive verification regime would also mean inspections of the biotechnology industry, a very important U.S. growth industry, where trade secrets are created with millions of dollars of investment and might easily be stolen or unwittingly compro-mised by inspectors.

These technical factors have led some experts to propose the creation of lists of biological agents and the definition of threshold quantities that, if exceeded, would constitute a violation. But vaccine production can require large quantities of agent—in the leadup to the ground war in the Persian Gulf, for example, it is likely that the United States had more an-thrax than Iraq because of its rush to inoculate its soldiers; but who was in violation of the BWC? The answer is Iraq because of the aggressive intent of its program. This points to the criterion of intent as a key discriminating factor in the biological domain, something that cannot easily be derived from dual-use facilities.

The clearest signal of offensive intent is the stockpiling of biological agent and weaponry. But, as argued above, the biotechnology revolution has made this less necessary. Indeed, stockpiling weapons implies a decision to hold them in abeyance, meaning probably for defensive or retaliatory purposes, and some proliferators may plan simply to produce and use biological weapons without lengthy stockpiling, much as Iraq's cw program seems to have been structured. Furthermore, for strategic uses atop missiles, a bw stockpile could be kept small and buried; once sufficient quantities of weapons for existing delivery vehicles are produced, the entire research, development, and production infrastructure could be dismantled (although periodic replenishment of the agent would probably be necessary given that most bw agents are not long-lived under such conditions). To complicate the verification challenge even further, weaponization is not the sine qua non of a militarily significant bw program. Other strategic applications include attack on agriculture or livestock. Delivery by unconventional means is also possible—via vectors such as insects and birds.

Because the CWC embodies a laboriously worked out approach to the balance between systematic and challenge inspections, it is a model worth exploring for the BWC. But its provisions cannot be fitted formalistically to the BWC. CWC negotiators have carefully matched the exigencies of systematic and challenge inspections to the technical characteristics of the chemical industry (through the three schedules of chemicals and their different monitoring provisions) and to considerations of the military significance of various types of capabilities (through a system with higher confidence in detecting stockpiles and production facilities than R&D for offensive purposes). This is backed up by a system of data exchanges and by a careful reading of what is also necessary to ensure that commercial or military secrets not relevant to the purposes of the treaty are not compromised.

Simply lifting these provisions into the BWC does not make sense. Indeed, nowhere in the U.S. arms control experience is there an example of simply applying a verification regime worked out for one treaty to another. Were BWC adherents to decide to require declarations of all facilities engaged in bw work, or capable of such, and to require their systematic inspection, a valuable benchmark would be gained, going well beyond the CBMs. But such inspections would be less effective than those in the chemical, nuclear, and conventional areas at ensuring that countries would not engage in bw activities of an offensive and militarily significant nature, for the reasons given above. Challenge inspections at both declared and undeclared facilities would thus have even more importance under the BWC, but they too would have lower probabilities of catching malefactors than in the chemical domain.

The problems associated with inspections thus led the United States to argue repeatedly at the Third Review Conference that the BWC was not verifiable and to emphasize the CBM agenda. Asserting that its views were well founded in many years of arms control verification work far more extensive than that of virtually any other BWC signatory, the United States essentially maintained that what can be monitored under the BWC is not very important, and that what cannot be monitored could be militarily critical. It also argued that even an effective verification regime should not be implemented if the costs outweighed the benefits. Such costs could include not just the fiscal drain but also the loss of legitimately sensitive or proprietary information—and even the possible erosion of political will to pursue compliance concerns in those instances where such inspections fail to produce unambiguous evidence of cheating. The United States also doubts the political acceptability of intrusive inspections in countries with advanced biotechnology industries and among those authoritarian, closed countries of the developing world that view inspections generally as anathema to national sovereignty and that are also the countries of most concern with regard to proliferation. To put a finer point on the argument, the United States held to the view that it had not yet been able to identify any means by which to accomplish BWC verification at reasonable cost. This position leaves the door open to further debate.[42]

Other developed countries participating in the BWC debate seem to have coalesced around a view that some mechanism to conduct challenge inspections to determine BWC compliance would be a valuable adjunct and is feasible at reasonable cost. The Europeans argue that, by posing a reasonable chance of detection, such a mechanism would have a significant deterrent effect upon states contemplating a bw program or an expansion of R&D into a stockpile. They cite the UNSCOM experience in Iraq, where inspections of a suspect bw site were sufficient to compel Iraq to admit its offensive program, concluding that verification would be useful for deterring, obstructing, postponing, or otherwise forcing a temporary discontinuation of bw programs.[43] Europeans also tend to be less concerned about the risks of compromising commercial secrets because they have worked under foreign inspectors (for example, from the U.S. Food and Drug Administration) in order to gain access to the pharmaceutical markets in various nations.

The transatlantic debate has been sharp on these issues, but it hardly encompasses the full range of views that must be included in any refashioning of the BWC. States of the developing world must also be heard. In general over the years, and with a few notable exceptions, their interest in the BWC has been noteworthy mostly for its absence. At the Third Review Conference, this attitude was beginning to change. It is important to note that the commitment of the nonaligned states to the BWC is not tempered by the double standard that applies in the nuclear domain, where under the Nuclear Non-Proliferation Treaty (NPT) the right to possess nuclear weapons has been retained by those who had them before 1967; the BWC, in contrast, is intended to disarm everyone.

An element of obstructionism is evident, however. Some developing countries see the BWC primarily as a way to boost their economic development through assistance in the biotechnical area. The price for their future support of the convention may prove to be increased assistance. But the developed countries are loath to spare this both for fiscal reasons and because of the bw proliferation risks associated with the spread of dual-use technologies.

The key outstanding points of dispute on the verification subject are being addressed by an expert group empaneled after the Third Review Conference. Dismissed by some as an attempt by a beleaguered Bush administration to buy time on the issue, the experts group exercise reflects a worthy effort to isolate the BWC verification subject from the fervor generated by the events of 1990 and 1991 and to evaluate, in a non-polemical way and without haste, the limits of various verification methods. It is unlikely that agreement will ever be reached on how much verification is enough and at what cost, on how the risk of being caught might be weighed as a significant probability by cheaters, and on whether increasing the perceived costs of cheating will also translate into high confidence in the regime. But some coalescence of views is likely, and it is reasonable to expect the adoption of some verification measures at the next review conference.

This will require some evolution in the thinking of the United States on BWC verification. But a precedent for this can be found in the cw domain, where steady international political pressure and leadership from senior levels of the Bush administration propelled a tortuous review of U.S. thinking on cw verification that ultimately meant real changes in policy. It will also require some tempering of the transatlantic debate, where in any case it seems that each party has overstated its case somewhat in order to secure concessions by the other. Bold statements like "the treaty is not verifiable" and "something is better than nothing" will lose their impact once experts have done their homework and defined exactly what is and is not verifiable and with what degree of confidence. Only at this point will it be possible to weigh the costs of attempting to incorporate new measures against the costs of not doing so—especially with regard to proliferation.

It is essential that verification issues should not become the sole vehicle for seeking greater compliance with the BWC. Verification measures are talked about today as if they were a quick fix for the regime. They are not. Verification is only an instrument of compliance policy. The credibility of verification measures as a deterrent will be greatly enhanced if key interested states are engaged politically. The ultimate impact of such measures will depend almost entirely on whether the political will can be mustered when noncompliance is detected or, which will be more difficult, when doubts about noncompliance remain unresolved. For these larger compliance purposes, CBMs will continue to be useful.[44] Ad hoc mechanisms, such as UNSCOM and the tripartite U.S.-UK-Russian agreement, will also be helpful in resolving compliance concerns in instances where circumstances permit measures beyond those in a multilateral treaty.[45]

Indeed, the overall effectiveness of the arms control agenda will be bolstered significantly by steps taken in other areas, for example, export controls. The United States pursues such controls under the aegis of the Australia Group, which in 1989 expanded its mandate from cw to bw issues and since then has facilitated the implementation of controls on microorganisms and some especially sensitive technologies. A continued commitment to effective export controls and to coordination among countries engaged in such trade will be a priority for the foreseeable future.

Conclusion

This review illustrates the degree to which the challenges in the bw area have grown more pronounced in the last two decades. The proliferation of biological weapons has increased the risk that such weapons will be used in war, whether by states within regions in conflict or against intervening forces, or by non-state actors against states, ethnic groups, or targets of primarily political content. Such proliferation also accelerates the erosion of confidence in the Biological Weapons Convention set in motion by issues of noncompliance. The biotechnology revolution has heightened fears that the effort to ban biological weapons may succumb to technological innovation and changing capabilities. All of this is occurring against a background of growing international instability wrought by the end of the cold war, the proliferation of other unconventional and conventional military capabilities, and sharp international debate about how well collective security can operate in this new era. These factors combine to increase the likelihood that biological weapons will be used and to decrease the effectiveness of the policy approaches adopted in past decades.

But these problems should not be overdramatized. BW proliferation remains partial. The biotechnology revolution has eased some of the technical constraints on biological warfare but has hardly eliminated them. Disincentives to terrorist use of biological weapons remain. The treaty regime is under increasing stress but periodic review conferences have helped it to adjust to new realities and can be expected to do so in the future. Both global and regional arms control measures appear to be of growing importance politically and operationally as the tangible fear of biological warfare and weapons proliferation more generally has created new incentives for cooperative action. Relative to other issues of international security after the cold war and the Persian Gulf War, bw is ascending, but it is not at this time the type of priority requiring major departures of policy or investments of resources.

New policy approaches are nonetheless warranted. This requires a revision of military and arms control measures to keep abreast of changing times as well as a review at the level of national strategy so that these various instruments reinforce one another—and dovetail with those of U.S. international partners. Neither arms control nor military policies alone can eliminate the threat that biological weapons will be used against the United States, its allies, or their military forces. But if pursued in concert, arms control and military policies can work as a "web of deterrence"[46] to limit the extent of the problem and keep the most serious transgressors at bay.

On the military side, policy priorities should include improvement in the capacity to anticipate and evaluate biological threats and to survive and prevail in a biologically contaminated environment if compelled to fight there. This means more funding for, and organizational focus on, intelligence, detection gear, protective kits, and the means to attack bw assets preemptively or to defeat them once they are used. The most urgent short-term priority is to hear the alarm that rang in the Persian Gulf War—the risk of confronting biological weapons on the battlefield is real, and the United States cannot any longer neglect the minimal tasks of bw preparedness, that is, fielding adequate detectors and protective gear and preparing vaccines for known bw agents.

U.S. interests continue to be well served by the country's refusal to possess biological weapons. A renewed capacity for in-kind retaliation would add little to the U.S. force posture; the cost of acquiring such a capability would be abandonment of the Biological Weapons Convention, which would stimulate proliferation and increase the military threat.

The bw problem reinforces other priorities in U.S. defense and security policy. It increases the salience of retaining nuclear options while also augmenting conventional ones. It underscores the value of conventional preponderance, force mobility, and dispersed warfare in deterring and defeating attack on U.S. forces with unconventional weapons. It also highlights the importance of using force abroad only when backed by clear political will. Without a clear expression of that will, the United States risks bw attack by those who calculate its commitment to be weak and thus susceptible to one terrorizing blow.

On the arms control side, continued strengthening of the BWC is an increasingly important priority. The international process of study and evaluation that is under way should be encouraged, and a verification regime should be adopted if one can be shown to be effective, politically acceptable, and not unduly costly.

But arms control in the biological area is not a panacea. Having the means to detect and deter noncompliance is only part of the compliance challenge. A more effective regime requires continued diplomatic efforts, led by key interested states parties, to more fully engage their fellow participants.

The BWC is only a tool of policy, as are military programs. With meaningful political commitment they can be used to ameliorate the bw problem; used badly or not at all, they can make the problem much more severe. Such commitment exists today only episodically in the West and hardly ever in the developing world. The bw issue cannot remain a backwater of public policy. To ignore issues related to the control of biological weapons and the deterrence of biological warfare would be to condemn the international community in decades hence to negative trends that today are by no means inexorable.

Notes

1. See SIPRI, *The Problem of Chemical and Biological Warfare,* vol. 2, *CB Weapons Today* (Stockholm: Stockholm International Peace Research Institute, 1973) for a detailed introduction to the agents and character of biological warfare.

2. The United States, along with many other Geneva Protocol signatories, has reserved for itself the right to use chemical weapons in retaliation if another state initiates chemical warfare. No such reservation was filed for biological weapons. The United States ratified its adherence to the Protocol only in 1975, at a time when chemical weapons remained in its arsenal but after it had unilaterally renounced its right to any use of biological weapons (in 1969).

3. Peter Williams and David Wallace, *Unit 731: Japan's Secret Biological Warfare in World War II* (New York: Free Press, 1989). See also Tracy Dahlby, "Japan's Germ Warriors," *Washington Post,* May 26, 1983, pp. A–1, 25.

4. See in this volume Thomas Dashiell, "A Review of U.S. Biological Warfare Policies," and Graham S. Pearson, "Biological Weapons: The British View."

5. For a review of various policy perspectives on the cbw problem of the late 1960s, see *Chemical-Biological Warfare: U.S. Policies and International Effects,* Hearings Before the Subcommittee on National Security Policy and Scientific Developments of the Committee on Foreign Affairs, U.S. House of Representatives, November 18, 20; December 2, 9, 18, and 19, 1969 (Washington, D.C.: GPO, 1970).

6. See in this volume Dashiell, "A Review of U.S. Biological Warfare Policies." See also Charles Piller and Keith R. Yamamoto, *Gene Wars: Military Control Over the New Genetic Technologies* (New York: Beech Tree Books/William Morrow, 1988).

7. *Report of the Chemical Warfare Review Commission* (Washington, D.C.: GPO, June 1985), 71.

8. U.S. General Accounting Office, "Chemical Warfare: Soldiers Inadequately Equipped and Trained to Conduct

Chemical Operations," GAO/NSIAD-91-197 (Washington, D.C., May 1991). See also "Critical GAO Report on Chemical Attack Readiness Suppressed by Pentagon," *Defense Week,* April 22, 1991, p. 5.

9. See in this volume Seth Carus, "The Proliferation of Biological Weapons," and Pearson, "Biological Weapons: The British View."

10. For a review of bw allegations, see Elisa D. Harris, Statement to the Defense, Foreign Policy, and Space Task Force of the Budget Committee of the U.S. House of Representatives, May 22, 1991.

11. See testimony by the then-director of the Central Intelligence Agency, William H. Webster, of February 9, 1989, in *Global Spread of Chemical and Biological Weapons,* Hearings Before the Committee on Governmental Affairs and Its Permanent Subcommittee on Investigations, U.S. Senate, February 9–10, May 2, 17, 1989.

12. See "General Quizzed on Chemical Weapons Production," *Izvestia,* in Foreign Broadcast Information Service— Soviet Union-92-082, April 28, 1992.

13. See in this volume Carus, "The Proliferation of Biological Weapons." See also "Iraqi CBW Armament and the UN Special Commission," *Chemical Weapons Convention Bulletin,* no. 13 (September 1991): 21–22.

14. R. Jeffrey Smith, "Agency Gets Last Word on Poison Gas," *Washington Post,* December 13, 1989, describes a dispute between outgoing ACDA director William F. Burns and the administration on the number of developing countries whose cw programs are militarily significant.

15. See in this volume Victor Utgoff, "The Biotechnology Revolution and Its Potential Military Implications." See also Brad Roberts, "Chemical and Biological Weapons: New Technology and the Prospects for Negotiations," in Kenneth B. Moss, ed., *Technology and the Future Strategic Environment* (Washington, D.C.: Wilson Center Press, 1990), 1–24. See also *Global Spread of Chemical and Biological Weapons,* particularly the hearings of May 17, 1989, which focused on bw proliferation and the new genetics.

16. For a discussion of the connection between technological change and military utility, see Jonathan B. Tucker, "The Future of Biological Warfare," in W. Thomas Wander and Eric H. Arnett, eds., *The Proliferation of Advanced Weaponry: Technology, Motivations, and Responses* (Washington, D.C.: American Association for the Advancement of Science, 1992), 53–73.

17. Testimony of Thomas Welch, deputy assistant secretary of defense (chemical matters), as reported in *Defense Week*, May 9, 1988.

18. See "Potential for Use by Terrorists of Binary Weapons," in *Binary Weapons: Implications of the U.S. Chemical Weapons Stockpile Modernization Program for Chemical Weapons Proliferation*, Report prepared for the Subcommittee on International Security and Scientific Affairs, Committee on Foreign Affairs, U.S. House of Representatives, April 24, 1984.

19. See in this volume Robert Kupperman and David Smith, "Coping With Biological Terrorism."

20. See the three policy papers published on this subject by the Washington Institute for Near East Policy: Seth Carus, *The Genie Unleashed: Iraq's Chemical and Biological Weapons Production*, no. 14 (1989); Mike Eisenstadt, *The Sword of the Arabs: Iraq's Strategic Weapons*, no. 21 (1990); and Carus, *"The Poor Man's Atomic Bomb?" Biological Weapons in the Middle East*, no. 23 (1991).

21. U.S. Department of State, *Chemical Warfare in Southeast Asia and Afghanistan, Special Report No. 98* (Washington, D.C., March 22, 1982). See also U.S. Defense Intelligence Agency, *Soviet Chemical Weapons Threat*, DST-1620F-051-85 (Washington, D.C., 1985).

22. Julian Robinson, Jeanne Guillemin, and Matthew Meselson, "Yellow Rain: The Story Collapses," *Foreign Policy*, no. 68 (Fall 1987): 100–117.

23. Ann Devroy and R. Jeffrey Smith, "U.S., Russia Pledge New Partnership," *Washington Post*, February 2, 1992, p. A–1.

24. Interview, *Komsomolskaya Pravda*, May 27, 1992.

25. AP Executive News Service, September 23, 1992.

26. Statement by General Valentin Yevtigeneyev, deputy chief of the radiation, chemical, and biological protection

department of the Ministry of Defense, cited in AP Executive News Service, "Russia Ends Biological Weapons Program," September 14, 1992.

27. "U.S. Wants Russia to Reveal Germ Warfare Program," *Baltimore Sun*, March 22, 1992. Also, "16 Biological Weapons Sites Identified in ex-Soviet Union," *Washington Times*, March 3, 1992, p. 3.

28. R. Jeffrey Smith, "Russia Agrees to Inspection of Its Biological Research Facilities," *Washington Post*, September 15, 1992.

29. Although Russian authorities have confirmed that the 1979 anthrax deaths were tied to activities of a military nature at a biological research facility, debate continues about exactly what happened and why. Some recent investigators have described a pattern of events consistent with what might have happened if there had been a breach of a facility designed to test vaccines. Others have reported myriad explanations, including a railyard accident involving transport vessels containing large quantities of bw agent.

30. As one commentator has argued, "the steps in 'defensive' BW R&D are indistinguishable from the steps in 'offensive' BW R&D. Thus the presence of a 'defense' is fundamentally destabilizing and will almost certainly be perceived as a threat, triggering a parallel response." Jonathan King, "The Threat and Fallacy of a Biological Arms Race," *geneWATCH* 2, no. 2 (May-August 1985): 16, a special issue on the Military and the New Biology of the *Bulletin of the Committee for Responsible Genetics*. Some have urged expelling from professional associations any scientist engaged in a bw research program. See "Controversy Grows Over Pentagon's Work on Biological Agents," *Wall Street Journal*, September 17, 1986, p. 1.

31. See in this volume Dashiell, "A Review of U.S. Biological Warfare Policies." See also Lois Ember, "Threat of Chemical, Biological Arms in Post-Cold-War Era Assessed," *Chemical & Engineering News*, November 9, 1992, p. 23.

32. See in this volume David Huxsoll, "The U.S. Biological Defense Research Program."

33. World Health Organization, *The Work of WHO, 1988–1989: Biannual Report of the Director General to the World Health Assembly and the United Nations* (Geneva, 1990).

34. See in this volume Kupperman and Smith, "Coping With Biological Terrorism."

35. Baker Spring of the Heritage Foundation argues in favor of this option. See "Four Principles for Curtailing the Proliferation of Biological and Chemical Arms," Heritage Foundation Backgrounder no. 844 (Washington, D.C., August 19, 1991).

36. For a detailed analysis of the debate about the most effective way to deter chemical attack on U.S. forces, see Brad Roberts, *Chemical Disarmament and International Security*, Adelphi Paper no. 267 (London: Brassey's for IISS, 1992).

37. James Leonard, "Reviewing the Biological Weapons Convention," *Issues in Science and Technology* (Fall 1986): 12–13.

38. "Second Review Conference of the Biological Weapons Convention," *Disarmament* 10, no. 1 (Winter 1986/87): 43–72.

39. See in this volume Michael Moodie, "Arms Control and Biological Weapons." See also Nicholas Sims, "Achievements and Failures at the Third Review Conference," *Chemical Weapons Convention Bulletin*, no. 14 (December 1991): 2–5.

40. For a review of the verification topic in the context of the history of the BWC, see Barend ter Haar, *The Future of Biological Weapons* (New York: Praeger and CSIS, 1991). For a review of the BWC verification issue current to winter 1992, see Oliver Thränert, ed., *The Verification of the Biological Weapons Convention: Problems and Perspectives* (Bonn: Friedrich Ebert Stiftung, 1992).

41. See in this volume Huxsoll, "The U.S. Biological Defense Research Program."

42. A private initiative by the Federation of American Scientists has described the elements of a possible verification regime. See "Proposals for the Third Review Conference of the Biological Weapons Convention" (Washington, D.C., September 1990) and "Implementation of the Proposals for a Verification Protocol to the Biological Weapons Convention" (Washington, D.C., February 1991). These proposals, although not adopted by the U.S. government or the review conference,

helped to sharpen the debate about effectiveness and cost. See also Barbara Hatch Rosenberg and Gordon Burck, "Verification of Compliance with the Biological Weapons Convention," in Susan Wright, ed., *Preventing a Biological Arms Race* (Cambridge, Mass.: MIT Press, 1990), 300–329.

43. See a working paper prepared for the British delegation to the second BWC verification experts meeting entitled "UN Special Commission BW Inspections in Iraq: Lessons for the Ad Hoc Experts' Group on Verification," BWC/CONF.III/VEREX.WP5.

44. One proposal for a new CBM being debated in 1992 is the creation of an international project for vaccines research. It would have the twin purposes of drawing scientists into more collaborative, peaceful efforts while also providing vaccines where commercial incentives are not sufficient. The proposal has been criticized as entailing all of the proliferation risks of the similar Atoms for Peace initiative of four decades earlier. See Erhard Geissler and J. P. Woodall, eds., *Vaccines for Peace* (Stockholm: SIPRI, 1993). The proposal builds on a general approach emphasizing the confidence-building value of improved communication and trust among those individuals involved in the biological sciences, as well as a strong commitment to ethically justifiable work. See Erhard Geissler and Robert H. Haynes, *Prevention of a Biological and Toxin Arms Race and the Responsibility of Scientists* (Berlin: Akademie Verlag, 1991).

45. Smith, "Russia Agrees to Inspections of Its Biological Research Facilities."

46. See in this volume Pearson, "Biological Weapons: The British View." For a fuller explication of this concept, see Pearson, "Prospects for Chemical and Biological Arms Control: The Web of Deterrence," *The Washington Quarterly* 16 (Spring 1993).

CSIS BOOKS of Related Interest

Chemical Disarmament and U.S. Security
Brad Roberts, editor
July 1992   158 pp.   ____$37.50

This timely group of twelve essays is a superb primer on the CWC, rich with policy recommendations which should not be lost in the celebration over the signing of this historic agreement. In a concluding chapter, Roberts skillfully draws from the other essays to frame the upcoming ratification debate. If one has only enough time to read a single chapter, this should be it.--Review by John Parachini, *Arms Control Today*

This volume evaluates the merits of the Chemical Weapons Convention in terms of the security and national interests of the United States. It assesses U.S. policy options related to disarmament, nonproliferation, and military preparedness with an eye toward the upcoming Senate ratification debate on the Convention. Its contributors include a number of individuals from overseas whose views are not well known in the United States but help inform U.S. choices.

Contributors: Ronald F. Lehman, H. Martin Lancaster, Joachim Krause, Victor Utgoff and Susan Leibbrandt, W. Seth Carus, Trevor Wilson, Nabil Fahmy, Michael Krepon, John Walker, Kyle Olson, Charles C. Floweree, Brad Roberts

CSIS Copublished Book/Westview Press

Prospects for Cruise Missile Proliferation in the 1990s
W. Seth Carus
December 1992   172 pp.   ____$14.95 (pb)
                                                            ____$37.95 (hb)

Even before the Persian Gulf War, there was strong evidence to suggest a growing interest in cruise missiles by countries in the Third World. Until recently, Third World countries could not produce accurate, long-range guidance systems. This has started to change. This volume examines the evidence and includes an assessment of relative technological capabilities.

CSIS Washington Papers/Praeger

From CSIS Bookroom 1800 K Street, N.W. Suite 400 Washington, D.C. 20006

CSIS BOOKS of Related Interest

The Chemical Weapons Convention:
Implementation Issues
Brad Roberts, editor

January 1993   47 pp.   ___$8.95

"After nearly two decades of work under the aegis of the Conference on Disarmament in Geneva, diplomats have finalized a Chemical Weapons Convention, the purpose of which is a complete global ban on the production, stockpiling, and use of chemical weapons ....Whether the CWC emerges in future years as a useful instrument of international security, or turns out instead to be either irrelevant or counter productive, will be a direct function of how well policymakers build on the legal and organizational framework in the draft treaty with effective implementation policies."--H. Martin Lancaster, from the foreword

CSIS Significant Issues Series

The Future of Biological Weapons
Barend ter Haar
1991   190 pp.   ___$12.95 (pb)
                                                      ___$37.95 (hb)

The author, a Dutch diplomat with extensive disarmament experience, reviews the problem of biological welfare in the 20th century and discusses international efforts to ban such weapons. He analyzes various measures to strengthen the Biological Weapons Convention, emphasizing the work still needed to create a strong verifiable convention.

CSIS Washington Papers/Praeger

From CSIS Bookroom 1800 K Street, N.W. Suite 400 Washington, D.C. 20006

CSIS BOOKS of Related Interest

Congressional Oversight of National Security:
A Mandate for Change
John O. Marsh, project chairman
James Blackwell, project director
December 1992   29 pp.   ___$10.95

The shared power between the Congress and the executive branch as envisioned by the founding fathers in the Constitution is rapidly being obliterated by the changing geostrategic environment. Since the Vietnam War, congressional micromanagement of the defense establishment has grown phenomenally. A CSIS steering committee examined the causes and consequences and proposes a broad set of needed reforms.

CSIS Panel Report

Order Form

Postage and handling   _3.50_

All orders must be prepaid or charged.   **Total** _____

___ Check (payable to CSIS)

___ VISA ___ MASTERCARD   Exp. date _____

Card No. _____

Name on card _____

Signature _____

Send books to: _____

_____

_____

Send order to

From CSIS Bookroom 1800 K Street, N.W. Suite 400 Washington, D.C. 20006